Supporting Your Child with Special Needs

Supporting Your Child with Special Needs offers practical activities and strategies to help you prepare your children for school success and best connect with school personnel to meet your child's unique needs. Each of the ten chapters includes key themes supported by research as well as activities for you to complete with your children to bond with and build them up. Rachel Jorgensen's guidance will help you both understand and tackle the real-world situations you'll encounter as a parent navigating the special education system. You will find yourself better equipped to support your child in the school setting and better able to prepare your child for a path to greater independence in adulthood.

Rachel R. Jorgensen is a special educator, college instructor, and educational writer with a special interest in empowering learners with special needs. She has spent nearly 20 years in the special education classroom and continues to enjoy her daily work with her students.

T0373763

Other Eye On Education Books
Available From Routledge
www.routledge.com/k-12

Supporting Your Child with Special Needs

50 Fundamental Tools for Families

Rachel R. Jorgensen

Routledge
Taylor & Francis Group

NEW YORK AND LONDON

Designed cover image: © Getty Images

First published 2023
by Routledge
605 Third Avenue, New York, NY 10158

and by Routledge
4 Park Square, Milton Park, Abingdon, Oxon, OX14 4RN

Routledge is an imprint of the Taylor & Francis Group, an informa business

© 2023 Rachel R. Jorgensen

ISBN: 9781032428192 (hbk)
ISBN: 9781032425238 (pbk)
ISBN: 9781003364443 (ebk)

DOI: 10.4324/9781003364443

Typeset in Palatino
by codeMantra

Access the Support Material: www.routledge.com/9781032425238

To all the parents loving their children with all their might and to my wonderful people: Bennett, Samri and Adam, Lori, Randy, Melanie, Aaron, Brynn and Eli. You make me a better mom every day.

Contents

Disclaimer

First and foremost, let me say that I have no idea what it is like to be in your shoes, and neither does anyone else. The experience of parenting is unique to every individual, and parenting a child with special needs is a profoundly rewarding, challenging, and multifaceted lifestyle which does not fit into any prescribed 'norm' or 'box.' As you are reading this book, you may find yourself wanting to exclaim, "Yes! I love that activity and I can't wait to try it!" You may also find yourself wanting to scream, "That could never work in real life- You have no idea what it's like to be me!" Both of these responses are natural and welcome! Please take what you can from this book with the understanding that your adventure as a parent/guardian is your own. The tips, tools, strategies, and activities you gather along the way will be those which resound with your own wise heart. My hope is that you collect nuggets of truth, wisdom, help, and support as you read and enjoy the content. Know that although I have no idea what it is like to walk in your shoes, I have worked with countless families and seen them through some of the most challenging times in their lives with their children.

As you delve into this book, there are a few terms you will see often which require a definition. First, the term 'parent' refers to anyone who engages in the act of parenting. This includes guardians, grandparents, aunts, uncles, and whoever else is a part of the process of raising a child. The term 'child with special needs' refers to the unique, brilliant, original, and valuable human being who is experiencing the parenting process. Note that I am not a huge fan of the term 'special needs' because it has come to hold a stigma in many contexts. Essentially, this refers to the fact that the child qualifies for special education services in the school setting. That's it! The special education identifier is the ticket into a world of positive support and services which are meant to be a lifesaver for your family and your child. The term 'special needs' is broad for a reason, as the strategies in this book are intended to address a wide array of need areas.

Another important note as you begin to explore the tips, tools, research, and resources included here is that not everything will apply to you and your child. Read with an open mind and seek to find the items which best apply to your needs and/or the needs of your child. As a special educator nearing 20 years in the profession, I have worked with parents on varying ends of the 'burnout' spectrum. Some come to me frazzled and at the end of their rope disappointed by the school system and the demands of advocating for their child. Others arrive with fewer struggles, and yet, the need for ideas and information is there.

This book is a love letter to the beautiful act of raising a child with special needs. May it offer you energy, practically applicable tools, and most importantly, hope. As an educator and parent, I applaud you for investing the time to read material which could make a lasting positive impact for your family. Reading this book is ultimately an act of love. Thank you for showing up for your child in this manner!

Introduction

I'm so glad this book is in your hands. There is nothing more beautiful, messy, wonderful, difficult, and terrifying than being a parent. There is no handbook, no 'right' or 'wrong' way to do things, and no certainty in the act of parenting. Throw in the complexities involved in parenting a child with special education needs, and you have a recipe for even greater challenges. Thus, we arrive at the purpose of this book. My hope is that it brings you joy, energy, and some useful tips to help you enjoy your adventure as a parent navigating the world of special education along with your child.

Any parent can feel like a baby chick on the freeway at times. As a special education teacher for nearly 20 years, I have worked with countless families who are absolute champions for their children and who are also exhausted beyond measure. This book is intended to be a source of hope, strength, and knowledge to help you support your child through the experience of the special education system. The special education system is overwhelming (any way you slice it, especially if you try to read through the legislation – yikes!) and can add stress to your life as a parent. However, I believe that in actuality, special education is a beautiful gift the school system can offer to families and it can create powerful positive outcomes for students. The

> This book is intended to be a source of hope, strength, and knowledge to help you support your child through the experience of the special education system.

DOI: 10.4324/9781003364443-1

secret? Schools and families must find a way to connect and collaborate through authentic relationships. This book may provide just the bridge you need to make this connection.

As you read, my hope is that you will enjoy what this book has to offer. I encourage you to keep a light heart and don't stop smiling in all areas of your life, as a sense of humor can be pivotal to your happiness as a parent and a person. I have learned so much through a multitude of mishaps, errors, and mistakes in my work with families. We are all human beings, on all sides of the Individual Education Planning table. This book includes a collection of the lessons I have learned both as a special educator and as a mother which may help you actually enjoy your interactive experience with special education.

> We have the same goal: The success of your child.

Speaking as a special education teacher, I must say that this book is ultimately a work of my heart. I love my students and I know that their families love them too. We have the same goal: the success of the child. The avenues we would like to take to arrive at this goal may differ, and this is where conversation and collaboration come into play. My hope is that this book will open your eyes to the general process of special education and the ways it may open doors of opportunity for your child. I also hope that the family activities help you create a firm foundation of love and support to help your child thrive. So open your heart, open your mind, and happy reading!

Why Did I Write This Book?

I wrote this book for one simple reason: Gratitude. I am deeply grateful for every relationship I get to have with every parent and family. I spend up to 7.5 hours per day with my students at the absolute maximum. My role in their lives is only a very small slice of the pie. You as the parent know your child better than anyone on earth,

> You as the parent know your child better than anyone else, and thus, you are the most valuable expert on your child's needs.

and thus, you are the most valuable expert on your child's needs. Your participation in the special education process means that educators have the chance to tap into this expertise to help your child succeed. It's a beautiful thing, and for that I say: Thank You!

With this heart full of thanks, I offer this book as a resource for your family and your child. I have loaded it with tools to help you sustain yourself as a parent while offering your child a balance of love and accountability. In addition to addressing the special education system, I have included tools and tips to help build capacity in your child in other areas such as communication, self-advocacy, and self-management of undesirable behavior. As you build a peaceful home environment for your child, you are helping teachers more than you know. Note that I have tried to be as all-encompassing as possible, addressing the needs of families with an array of challenges and supporting learners across disability categories. Not all of the content will apply to you directly, but I believe that if you 'harvest the gold,' you will find invaluable content to transform your family life and your experience of the special education system.

What Will You Find in This Book?

The book begins with a focus on how the special education system works and how you might best connect with teachers and other legally required team members at school. This section will help you share helpful information about your child, encourage a focus on your child's strengths, walk through the Individual Education Planning process, and build skills for advocacy when this is needed. The activities will invite your child to understand the roles and responsibilities of educators and to help them share key information with their teachers through effective self-advocacy. Activities will also help you stay organized and aware through the Individual Education Planning process, offering ready-to-use items such as checklists, note-taking forms, and a team member directory. Finally, you will build your personal advocacy skills through activities focused on being proactive and using effective communication to ensure your voice is heard.

The second section of this book focuses on deepening your connection with your child. The first task any child seeks to accomplish is to have their basic needs met (Glasser, 2021). The first chapter will help you come together as a family to explore the basic needs which drive each of you and to identify what matters most to your child. Once the foundation is in place, you can explore the negative stories which have held you and/or your child back, co-creating a new story about what life and education could be. Another foundational element is a focus on strengths rather than difficulties and a new definition for the concept of 'success.' The hope is that progress, not perfection, becomes the focus in order to give both you and your child hope. This section also includes approaches and activities you can use when your relationship with your child is strained or there are struggles with challenging behaviors at times. Finally, the section closes with a chapter focused on coming together as a family unit built on acceptance, communication, shared positive attributes, and bright hopes for the future!

The final section of the book is focused on approaches you can use to take good, loving care of yourself as a parent. Your own health and wholeness may have a tremendous impact on your child's success. You will find strategies to exercise self-kindness, develop routines, uphold boundaries, and speak to yourself in a loving manner. At times, it is almost inevitable that things will go wrong and children may act out in response to difficult situations. This section provides tools you can use as a parent to sustain your deep love and commitment even when presented with such challenges. This section also includes tools to help you turn your day around when you feel upset or overwhelmed, cultivate authentic positivity, and make effective decisions. The section closes with a chapter focused on tools you can use to cultivate gratitude, change the things which are within your control, and accept the things which are not in your control. The final activity invites you to

> This book is all about POSSIBILITIES. For yourself, for your child, and for the beautiful future you can create together.

consider the beautiful legacy you hope to leave with your child as they move toward adulthood and build a life of their own.

This book is all about POSSIBILITIES. For yourself, for your child, and for the beautiful future you can create together. The content, resources, and strategies are designed to help you maintain your sense of motivation, commitment, and purpose every day. This book is 100% focused on the idea that you can thrive and live in peace as you parent your child with special education needs using the right mindset and approaches. After reading, you will find yourself better equipped to connect with the school and navigate the special education system with the knowledge to make full use of valuable opportunities. Also, it is my hope that you will feel energized to approach your role as parent with enthusiasm, joy, and love, determined to take steps to empower both yourself and your child.

Reference

Glasser, W. (2021). *Quality world: Choice theory, quality school, and classroom.* Glasser Institute. https://www.e-glasser.org/choice-theory-quality-school-and-classroom/.

I

Connecting with School

Welcome to part one of our journey: Connecting with School. I decided to start here for two reasons. First, as a special education teacher for nearly 20 years, I have much to share which may help you as a parent. Second, this is often the area of utmost concern for parents as they support their child with special education needs. The special education system is complex and it can be difficult to know exactly how to make the most of the resources available to help your child. Rest assured that this section is loaded with practical tools you can utilize to help you build a foundational relationship with school personnel, understand your legal rights, decipher the paperwork, and participate fully as a valued member of your child's Individual Education Planning team. Here you will also find strategies and activities to help you advocate for your child's needs and to equip them to advocate for themselves when needed. Happy reading!

DOI: 10.4324/9781003364443-2

1

The Foundational Relationship

Deanna Bradley was nervous. Her son Anthony would be starting middle school next week and she felt nothing but trepidation and worry. Elementary school had been tough for Anthony. He was able to keep up with the academic work, but he struggled with social skills and the school even identified him as having autism spectrum disorder. Deanna wasn't so sure, but she trusted the school and could see their point when it came to Anthony's struggles with social interaction, loud noises, rigid thinking and participating in groups. She agreed to special education services thinking that at least this would mean that all of the teachers would know about Anthony's needs. Now she wasn't so sure she'd made the right decision. Would Anthony experience bullying? Kids can be so mean. Would his teachers just see the autism spectrum disorder label and not her sweet, kind, capable little man? Would this actually result in success? She decided that all she could do was keep loving her child, communicating with the school, and keeping her eye out for any problems and issues. She would not be afraid to be a strong advocate for her son, expecting that teachers build on his strengths rather than focusing on his weaknesses.

Ms. Bradley's fears are not unique. When a student enters special education services, every parent moves through an emotional journey involving uncertainty and fear about what this could mean. Unfortunately, the stigmatization of students in special education continues to exist in school settings, even those which are striving to be most inclusive. While special education may unlock the door to needed help, it can also bring about subsequent undesirable experiences for students. You may identify with the question: "Will my child experience

> There is a whole world of hope and help waiting for your child in special education.

DOI: 10.4324/9781003364443-3

Key Themes

◆ The more you share information about your child's strengths, needs, preferences, and interests, the better school personnel can meet their needs.
◆ In order to encourage school personnel to focus on your child's strengths, share them! Identify them, discuss them with your child often, and pass this along to the school.
◆ As a parent, you can help your child understand the varying expectations of the school setting vs. other settings they experience.
◆ Defining the role of the student, teachers, and case managers can help your child understand what to expect and what to focus on each day at school.
◆ You won't always be there to share things with the teacher, so you can support your child in sharing key information using their own words and voices.

---

bullying? Will they be ostracized? Will they still receive a quality education which prepares them for adult life?"

Well, fear not! I'm not trying to frighten you or focus on the negative. There is a whole world of hope and help waiting for your child in special education. As a teacher and parent, I have always strived to see the person and view the disability as one of the many characteristics possessed by the child. It's just one piece of the elaborate puzzle which makes that child who they are. This chapter will help you celebrate and share your wonderful, unique, valuable little person with school personnel. The content and activities will invite you to help identify and share your child's strengths, interests, preferences, and needs. They will also help you empower your child to share this information on their own in order to support independence.

Labels Are for Soup Cans

Stroll down the aisles of any grocery store and you will find thousands of labels which tell you what is inside of each can, bottle package, and box. Nutritional labels are so detailed that you can discover exactly what is inside of your favorite foods, for better or for worse. You can trust that when you open that can of chicken noodle soup, you will find chicken noodle soup inside. Every Single Time. When it comes to identification for special

> Special education identification is simply a ticket in the door to a world of support and services your child can now access to improve the likelihood of success.

education services, the 'label' or 'category' selected for your child serves a very different function. Rather than explaining who your child is or reducing them to a simple set of characteristics, special education identification is simply a ticket in the door to a world of support and services your child can now access to improve the likelihood of success. This can be a gift. This can be a lifeline. This should not be a life sentence or a detriment to your child in any way.

Over my years in special education, I have learned that the label assigned to a student says nothing about who they are. Each learner is unique, significant, and possesses their own strengths along with their needs. As a parent, you can support your child by helping them identify their positive qualities, perspectives, interests, hopes, and dreams, and then sharing this information with school personnel. Essentially, you can help your child figure out who they are, celebrate themselves, and share this information at school. Rather than starting with their struggles and deficits, this helps everyone involved to fully see and empower your child.

Too often, children are aware of the labels the outside world has put on them. We all endure the pain of being stereotyped and this is a part of the human experience. The pain of unfair bias can be even more acute for our children after they arrive in the world of special education. We must help children learn that they are so much more than a label or a stereotype assigned to them by the outside world. They have an invaluable core identity made up of positive qualities, even if they don't believe this or the good stuff is hard to find!

> We must help children learn that they are so much more than a label or a stereotype assigned to them by the outside world.

The ultimate hope is that you as a parent and the child's support team at school (teachers, administrators, interventionists, etc.) can help the child realize that their personal identity is multifaceted and complex. They are respectable, unique individuals

This is ME!

"Be yourself . . . everyone else is taken" -Oscar Wilde		
SKILLS	PERSONALITY TRAITS	FAMILY MEMBERS
FAVORITES	PHOTO OR DRAWING OF ME:	TALENTS
PROUDEST MOMENT		GOALS
DREAMS	STRENGTHS	FUN FACT

who can decide who they want to be despite any negative messages they have received from others. Activity 1, 'This is Me,' offers your child the chance to describe who they are and capture a 'snapshot' you can share with school personnel to set things off on the right foot. Consider bringing this along to your first Individual Education Planning meeting and inviting your child to share about it.

Strengths-Based Special Education

As a special education teacher, I can offer you insights about how educators wrestle with our own biases which can relate to various disability areas. Too often, we come to expect a particular set of behaviors or characteristics based on what we learn about our students on paper. As you build a relationship with teachers at school, you help educators move beyond unfair biases when you consistently share about who your child is as a person and highlight their strengths. In my experience, special educators are THRILLED to learn about the strengths in their students, and you as a parent know these better than anyone. Consider this story about a young special educator who overcame some of his own biases to truly connect with a student living with autism spectrum disorder:

> Mr. Beckett was pretty excited about his job as a high school special education teacher at a large high school. It just so happened that his school offered a special program for students with autism spectrum disorder, and many of these students would be included in his classes. His nephew had Autism, so Mr. Beckett figured he knew exactly what to expect from his students. His nephew was quiet, withdrawn, and needed a lot of space. He expected that his students would be the same way, expecting them to prefer limited interaction. Mr. Beckett would just give them worksheets to complete instead of trying to get them to talk during class discussions.
>
> When Mr. Beckett took a peek at the paperwork for his caseload, he found himself growing a little more nervous. One

of the students flipped a desk in seventh grade. Sure, it was a long time ago, but it must be relevant if it still showed up in the paperwork. Guess that students must be pretty violent. Another student had a problem with aggression toward staff members if she didn't get her way. The list of issues went on, and the more he read the paperwork, the more concerned he got about helping the students. They seemed to have a lot of needs, and Mr. Beckett wasn't sure he had the skills to meet them in his new role.

Before meeting the students, he asked to meet with the Autism Specialist in his building, Ms. Lewis, to chat about the best approaches. She reassured him that she had worked with many of the students over her years in the district and that the students were actually fabulous!

"Look," she said, "Don't let the paperwork scare you. Some things need to be documented for legal reasons, but once school gets going, you will get into the groove and everything will be fine."

"Okay, that really helps. I actually have a nephew with Autism, so I know what they're like," Mr. Beckett replied.

"Um- wait a minute- 'what they're like'… what do you mean by that?" Asked Ms. Lewis, with concern in her tone.

"You know, quiet, withdrawn, isolated… stuff like that."

Ms. Lewis winced a bit, took a deep breath, and offered him a warm and knowing smile. With patient, careful words, she shared: "One thing I learned early on in my career is that if you've met a kid with autism, you've met ONE kid with Autism. The label might mean that there are some common trends, but every single student is SO unique. There is no way to know what a student will be like based on a label. I think the best thing you could do right now is open your mind and be the best teacher you can be for ALL of your students. Don't let the paperwork and the label stuff cloud your vision of the actual kid. The label is just the kid's ticket to the services they need and nothing more."

"Gotcha… that's actually really helpful!" Mr. Beckett said. As he reflected, he realized that he definitely felt ready to approach the class with an open mind.

The first day of school, as his students filed in, Mr. Beckett kept his eye out for his students with the 'bigger' behaviors in the past so he could try to help them feel comfortable. However, as he got going with the day's activities it sort of slipped his mind. The day was actually a blast! He focused on getting to know each student with some cheesy games, and everyone actually liked it. As the final bell rang and the students left, he sat down at his desk and smiled to himself, satisfied that he had done his best and that the students had enjoyed their first day.

Then, Mr. Beckett had a realization. He had totally forgotten about the students with the major behaviors in the past. None of his students jumped out at him as having big time issues. Sure, there were some unique students in each of his groups, but that's a good thing! Everybody seemed cool with each other and the day just generally felt good. From that day on, Mr. Beckett released his preconceived notions and expectations. He was delighted to find that his students were amazing, capable and extremely different from each other. There was no cookie-cutter version of a 'student with autism' based on something someone once researched or wrote about in a book. He treated all students with the same care, respect and support, building a trusting relationship with each one. Students thrived, and Mr. Beckett completely changed his perspective on labels and pre-existing notions on how students will behave.

Reading this story as a parent, you may feel a wide range of emotions. You may feel enraged and indignant about the stereotypes Mr. Beckett shared which was based on ONE example of a child with a disability in his life. You may feel excited about Ms. Lewis and her expert guidance. One guideline I would love to see you follow as I read insider tales from the school system is this: Any response is the right response. I am going to share with candor and honesty, understanding that at times you may find the information surprising. The truth of the matter is this: 99.9% of the teachers and school staff I have worked with over the years truly love students and are trying to do their very best! Bias, insensitive moments, and imperfection are part of the humanity of every employee at every school in every district everywhere. School personnel are human beings, not robots, and try as they might to keep all of their work and conversations positive, at times their messiness will shine through. The stories I share can help give you insights as to how to better connect with school staff, sometimes offering them grace to be human beings trying their best.

The specific vignette involving Mr. Beckett and Ms. Lewis is not unique in the world of special education. In my career as a special education teacher, I have read countless files on incoming students which include tremendous struggles, negative incidents, and dysfunction. I have scoured the paperwork for information on student strengths, preferences, and interests and found very little. This is a problem. As you participate in the special education process as a parent, you can help highlight your child's wonderful strengths and request that these be included throughout the paperwork. The most helpful, well-written Individual Education Plan will be peppered with student strengths.

> As you participate in the special education process as a parent, you can help highlight your child's wonderful strengths and request that these be included throughout the paperwork.

Research supports the importance of strengths-based education. Your efforts to include your child's strengths throughout the special education process will not be in vain. In fact, the disability itself may become a strength when we realize how it creates resilience, perseverance, and unique perspectives in your child. Scholars have argued that educators can best practice asset-based instruction that views students' differences as a strength, countering the more widespread view that inordinate achievement disparities stem from deficiencies in the child (Lopez, 2017). Both teachers and students benefit when they start each day, each lesson, each meeting, and each task with a focus on the strengths and assets they already possess. This can create a shift from a deficit mindset to one of celebration and gratitude.

> We can always choose to focus on the good in situations, and to build on what is already going well to improve areas of need.

I Am Strong

Recognizing your GOOD QUALITIES, or STRENGTHS is important. Read the
following list of strengths and circle at least FIVE which apply to you.
Not sure what a word means? Look it up! Don't see your strength? Fill in your own in the
blank spaces! Then, share this with your case manager as they get to know you. This can
help them support your success!

Creative	Inquisitive	Meticulous	Honest	Curiosity	Insightful
Friendly	Imaginative	Determined	Focused	Imaginative	Organized
Devoted	Honest	Insightful	Balanced	Diligent	Gentle
Happy	Helpful	Easygoing	Realistic	Nurturing	Thoughtful
Patience	Funny	Eloquent	Confident	Respectful	Self Control
Persistence	Forgiving	Assertive	Funny	Grateful	Brave

Complete the following to analyze each strength:

Strength 1: _____ How does this help me?
_____
_____

How can I use this even more in my life? _____
_____
_____
_____

Strength 2: _____ How does this help me?
_____
_____

How can I use this even more in my life? _____
_____
_____
_____

Strength 3: _____ How does this help me?
_____
_____

How can I use this even more in my life? _____
_____
_____
_____

Strength 4: _____ **How does this help me?**

_____

_____

How can I use this even more in my life? _____

_____

_____

_____

Strength 5: _____ **How does this help me?**

_____

_____

How can I use this even more in my life? _____

_____

_____

_____

As a parent, you play a key role in setting the stage for this kind of practice at school. Your piece of the puzzle? Identify and highlight your child's strengths prior to any interaction with school personnel. Then, talk about these strengths from the very first minute of the very first interaction of the very first day you connect with school personnel. This is particularly important with your child's case manager. You can set the tone for positive discourse about your child, no matter how difficult school experiences have been or how much you struggle with your child's challenging needs. We can always choose to focus on the good in situations and to build on what is already going well to improve areas of need. Activity 2 offers an activity entitled 'I am Strong' which invites you and your child to work together to identify areas of strength and reflect on how they have been helpful in the past. Taking the time to complete and share this form can provide an easy jumping-off point for strengths-based conversations at school, and who doesn't like easy!?

> It is so important to frame conversations about education in a positive light whenever possible.

As parents, we are human too. We don't wake up in the morning singing songs of praise for our child. Sometimes, I find my own children at home far more challenging than the students I work with at

My Child's Strengths

Complete this form and share it with your child's IEP team to help them bring out the BEST

at school!

Positive Attributes:

Five characteristics I love about my child:

1. _____
2. _____
3. _____
4. _____
5. _____

Gifts and Talents:

My child enjoys or is very good at:

_____
_____
_____
_____

Celebrations:

A time when my child really made me smile me was:

_____
_____
_____
_____

Happy Memories:

Some of my happiest memories with my child are:

_____
_____
_____
_____
_____
_____
_____
_____

school. Why? Because as parents we are so deeply invested in our children, it can sometimes hurt even more when they act out or push us away or neglect to follow our directions, etc. Parenting can be completely exasperating and overwhelming, which we will explore more deeply in Chapter 9 of this book. I have learned that no matter how stressed I may feel about my beautiful children, I can convey their positive attributes at school to set them up for success. I don't want my stress level to limit their ability to shine at school, so I try not to 'vent' or complain about my children to school personnel. I also don't 'vent' about school issues in front of my children. It is so important to frame conversations about education in a positive light whenever possible. Centering ourselves and returning to the positive can help both ourselves and our children.

The conversation about your child's strengths can sometimes become difficult when you are feeling exhausted or worn out as a parent. Guess what: You have full permission to inhabit this space. It is a completely natural part of being a parent and it is almost always temporary. To break out of that 'stuck' feeling when you are frustrated with your child, you can shift your focus to your child's strengths through intentional reflection. Activity 3 invites you to consider the characteristics you love about your child, special times with your child that make you smile, and your happiest memories. As you complete this exercise, you may enjoy reviewing photos or videos you may have saved over the years. It might also be a beautiful experience to share your responses with your child to deepen your connection. This experience can set the stage for you to share about your child's strengths with deeper conviction and authenticity. It can also help you pause, breathe, and remember the absolute beauty of your ride with your child (which can sometimes feel like a rollercoaster!).

Defining Roles at School

The other day, I ran into the parent of a former student at the grocery store. Her oldest son had been on my caseload and received my services before graduating a few years earlier. After some small talk catching up with the parent, she asked how she could register her younger son for my class. I explained that my classes are technically services on a student's Individual Education Plan and thus, he could certainly enroll if the team feels he needs it.

"He doesn't have an IEP, thank GOODNESS," She said, "Such a pain."

This statement caught me off guard. As we continued to chat, she shared about the challenges she had faced with the special education system. As she shared, I came to realize that her struggles with special education were also related to the emotions her older son had to navigate as he worked with a case manager and participated in special education services. He felt defeated, different, and somehow less than his peers because he was identified for 'special ed.' This saddened my heart deeply in that I had been his case manager. I wish I could have helped him more, but I didn't know about his struggles. This also made me think about how parents and school personnel can work together to prevent some of these struggles.

> Special education is not a 'place,' but rather, it's a team of support available to help. Nothing more. Framed in this way, what could be more positive?

I believe that if we take the time to clearly define roles and responsibilities so students know what to expect. Special education is not a 'place,' but rather, it's a team of support available to help. Nothing more. Framed in this way, what could be more positive? The first individual to identify and connect with is the case manager. This individual can be a pivotal relationship for your child which determines how they will experience special education. It can help your child tremendously to help them understand what to expect from their case manager. Essentially, the role of the case manager includes a series of tasks such as detailed in Table 1.1.

The better your child connects with their case manager, the more likely it is that they will make full use of this support at school. In addition to their case manager, your child may benefit from the support of teachers and educational assistants in the school setting. Again, the better they connect, the more likely it is that they will succeed. As a parent, you can help set the stage for success by speaking positively about school personnel as much as you can. Even if you feel frustrated, sharing this with your

TABLE 1.1 What Does a Case Manager Do?

Key Roles	Details and How It Helps You!
Write your Individual Education Plan	Have a meeting and write your Individual Education Plan: ◆ Include the things you are good at. ◆ Include how you are doing in school. ◆ Include the goals you want to work on.
Help you out when you need it.	Write up a plan to help school go well. Share the plan to make sure it happens. Offer support if you need a change to your plan. Offer support if you are struggling in any way. Offer support if you need help with your work.
Check in on how you're doing.	Keep track of your progress on your goals to help you. Keep an eye on your grades in your classes. Check in with parents/families often.

child may actually result in severed or strained relationships at school. As a parent, even if I disagree with a teacher's actions, words, or practices, I keep this to myself. If I share this with my child, I may be setting them up to say or do something which would cause or deepen division with this particular educator. Rather than voicing my negative opinions to my child, I opt to advocate as needed. In order to support my child best, I frame the conversation around what they can expect at school and what they can do to help themselves find greater success.

How can you help set your child up for success? You and your child can come together to define how things will play out on an ideal day for everyone. This takes the pressure off as it helps make everything clear and transparent. Research supports the idea that defining roles and expectations in the classroom can help everyone involved relax and enjoy the environment (Sprick, 2013). I truly believe that most problems students experience during the school day have a lot to do with miscommunication and a lack of clarity. We do best when we lay things out clearly for children, and we also help their teachers in the process.

'Student's Job, Teacher's Job' (Activity 4) is a tool you can use to make things crystal clear for your child to help them understand the roles and responsibilities they carry at school. There is a beautiful safety in that! You may choose to invite your student's

Student's Job, Teacher's Job

Complete this form with your child to help them understand their job at school. Feel free to share with IEP team members to support common understandings and define roles for success.

The student's job in the classroom	The teacher's job in the classroom
The student's job in the school.	**The case manager's job in the school**
Tasks students and teachers complete together . . .	

case manager or teacher into the conversation as you complete this form. The conversation may flow as follows:

- ◆ What do you think the teacher's job is in the classroom (or small group)? (Note your child's responses).
- ◆ Here are my ideas for the teacher's job in the classroom (or small group): (List your ideas for the teacher's role).
- ◆ What do you think the student's job is in the classroom (or small group)? (Note your child's response).
- ◆ Here are my ideas for the student's job in the classroom (or small group): (List your ideas).
- ◆ You also have a case manager at school. Here are my ideas about what that means: (List the responsibilities of a case manager, referencing Table 1.1 for help).
- ◆ Your case manager can help you at school, but you will be responsible for many tasks on your own during your school day. Here are my ideas about what you will be able to manage by yourself, although you can always ask your case manager for help if needed: (List tasks your child needs to complete or at least attempt without help such as following their schedule, paying attention in class, and attempting assignments).
- ◆ Identify tasks teachers and your child will complete together.

This practice can help your child understand expectations. It can also guard against overhelping, as it defines the limits of the teacher/case manager role. Research has shown that overhelping students, or offering assistance they don't actually require, can actually lower their self-esteem and limit them (Nario-Redmond et al., 2019). Use the 'Student's Job/Teacher's Job' process to encourage independence as much as possible!

A Foundation for Self-Advocacy

Your child will always have one very special person in their lives, with them wherever they go and at all times: Their own wonderful self! Thus, helping our children take charge of their own lives and find their own voices might be one of our most important tasks as a parent. As our children develop, we set them up to succeed when we invite them to speak for themselves. This includes advocating for themselves at school. Depending on the nature and impact of your child's disability, their level of self-advocacy skills will vary. However, ALL children benefit from a mindset in which we are fostering self-advocacy to the greatest extent possible. We will not always be there to speak for them, and they need to grow the ability to meet their own needs to the greatest extent possible if they are going to be prepared for lifelong success.

> Helping our children take charge of their own lives and find their own voices might be one of our most important tasks as a parent.

When children know how to advocate for themselves, they are better prepared for lasting success in the big, wide world. This also takes the pressure off of you as a parent to serve as a constant voice. It's beautiful when you realize that your child is practicing something at school which you taught them at home, and it is actually WORKING! Hooray! When we empower our children by encouraging them to stand up for what they need and use their own voices, we protect ourselves from burning out as parents. Our children take charge and we can step back, relax, and watch them succeed. Of course, we are always waiting in the wings should they need our help. Most often, once they realize that they can thrive and they learn to believe in themselves, they are able to exceed any limiting expectations.

Supporting your child in developing self-advocacy skills should begin very early in the education process. As mentioned, this starts by helping children recognize their personal strengths and assets. Next, our children must believe in their own potential. They need to understand themselves and what helps them find success at school. As you discuss this information, you can help your child find a voice regarding their learning needs to help their teachers and school staff understand them better. Activity 5 provides a structured form which allows you to carry on this conversation with your child. The prompts and questions

Things My Teachers Should Know . . .

Name: _____ Date: _____

I love it when teachers . . .

_____
_____

I don't like it when teachers . . .

_____
_____

I wish my teachers knew that . . .

_____
_____

One thing that is hard for me at school is . . .

_____
_____

My favorite thing about school this year is . . .

_____
_____

My favorite type of teachers are . . .

_____
_____

Please try to . . .

_____
_____

Please try not to . . .

_____
_____

The best way to help me learn is . . .

_____
_____

---

can both open conversations and help them find their voice. You might choose to share this form with their teachers and case managers to set the stage for success. Better yet, invite your child to share and discuss this with their teachers on their own.

Conclusion

And so it begins. Your child is on a journey in special education. The best foundation you can offer your child is a strong sense of who they are as they experience the special education services. It has nothing to do with any label anyone else has put on them, or any negative message they have received from an external source. Each day is a new day for them to create the person they want to be. It's a beautiful journey, and we get to be along for the ride with our children! Use the tools found in this chapter to identify and celebrate your child's strengths. These can become the driving force behind Individual Education Planning and conversations with school personnel.

You can also set the stage for a healthy and productive relationship between your child and school staff. Have a conversation about the roles and responsibilities held by school staff. Also make sure your child understands the tasks and actions expected of them at school. Often, children struggle at school because they aren't sure what they are supposed to do or they are confused. This leads them to act out and can put them in quite a pickle. You can help them understand roles through the use of the tools in this chapter. Finally, you can help your child find their voice. As they complete the activity entitled 'My Teacher Should Know,' they are putting words to struggles which could otherwise lead to undesirable behavior or challenges. As a parent, you will help your child shine as you engage them in knowing themselves, knowing their strengths, and knowing what they need to be successful.

Chapter 1 Simple Snapshot

♦ Your child has a unique, valuable, amazing identity worth sharing with the school.

- ◆ Your child possesses numerous strengths which help them every day, and these should drive Individual Education Planning conversations and programming.
- ◆ No matter how exhausted or tired you feel at times as a parent, refocusing on your child's strengths can help you feel energized and refreshed.
- ◆ No matter how much you dislike or disagree with a school staff member, it helps to keep these conversations between you and other adults, and not share this with your child to the greatest extent possible.
- ◆ You can help equip your child for success by defining roles and responsibilities in the education process. What do teachers do? What do case managers do? What do students do?
- ◆ Help your child find their voice by discussing their needs and preferences and how this coincides with their experiences at school.

Chapter 1 Reflection Questions

Use the following questions to reflect on what you have learned in the chapter. You may choose to journal about them or discuss them with a friend or book club.

1. What do you love most about your child? How might you best share this with the school?
2. What are some of the negative labels or words you have heard spoken about your child? How has this impacted your experience or the experience of your child?
3. How might you use the tools from this chapter to help your child find their true identity and strengths?
4. What might be some helpful results which could come from defining roles and responsibilities at school?
5. How is your child doing in the area of speaking up for themself at school? How might you help them grow in this area?

6. What might be some areas in your child's life in which you could encourage increased independence? Where might you be overhelping?

References

Lopez, F. (2017). Altering the trajectory of the self-fulfilling prophecy: Asset-based pedagogy and classroom dynamics. *Journal of Teacher Education*, vol. 68, no. 2, pp. 193–212, doi:10.1177/0022487116685751.

Nario-Redmond, Michelle R., Kemerling, A. and Silverman, A. (2019). Hostile, benevolent, and ambivalent ableism: Contemporary manifestations. *Journal of Social Issues*, vol. 75, no. 3, pp. 726–756, doi:10.1111/josi.12337.

Sprick, Randall S. (2013). *Discipline in the secondary classroom: A positive approach to behavior management*. Hoboken, NJ: John Wiley & Sons, Incorporated.

2
Navigating the Special Education System

In her heart, Maya Martin knew that there was something different about her child Max. Max had always been busy and was always on the go, but when he went to kindergarten, his struggle to sit still and pay attention to information became pronounced. Max's teachers reported that he seemed to be 'run by a motor' and couldn't seem to stop. At home this didn't seem like a problem. She loved her son's energy and half the time he was out and about with the neighborhood kids enjoying life.

By third grade, the school had serious concerns about Max, especially because he was struggling to complete multi-step problems in math class and he couldn't concentrate long enough to build his reading skills. His academics were falling behind and he was having trouble connecting socially because his peers seemed bothered by his exorbitant energy level. At times, he would get up and flee from the classroom without permission and without a clear reason, causing a safety concern. After a visit to the doctor and a medical evaluation, Max was diagnosed with attention-deficit hyperactivity disorder, something Ms. Martin had heard of frequently, but that she never imagined would be applied to her own child.

This was overwhelming and a bit scary, in all honesty. Ms. Martin started to read all she could about the diagnosis and how she could help her son. Based on the literature's suggestion, Ms. Martin decided to share this information with the school. Her timing was impeccable. The school support advocate shared that they were planning to request a special education evaluation for Max. This diagnosis would help inform the team and would probably help Max qualify for services to help him. Special education? Ms. Martin's mind reeled. Another unexpected turn in the life of her little man. Amid a swirl of emotions including fear, uncertainty and a faint whiff of hope, she agreed to attend a meeting to discuss the evaluation.

The day of the meeting, Ms. Martin hustled out of work early and thanked her boss for the flexibility with her schedule. She arrived at the school feeling

DOI: 10.4324/9781003364443-4

flustered and she wasn't sure where to go. A staff member met her at the door and asked her to have a seat in the office to wait for a special education staff member to come and meet her to walk her to the meeting room. So she sat. In the principal's office. Feeling uncertain, unprepared and somehow small. As the smiling special education teacher invited to walk down the hall for the meeting, Ms. Martin wished she could turn and bolt out the door herself. Instead, she made the conscious decision to breathe, go with the flow, and trust the process....

As a special educator, my heart is breaking for Ms. Martin. She is facing so much uncertainty, so much confusion, and so many unknowns, all while trying to love and support the child she adores. Perhaps her story sounds familiar to you. Perhaps you have even had to sit in the 'principal's office' waiting for that first meeting filled with too much information and too many acronyms. It can all feel like far too much. This chapter is designed to help you understand the special education process in a nutshell, explore the Individual Education Planning (IEP) process, and ask key questions to secure the help you need for your child. The activities include tools to keep track of key team members/resources, steps in the IEP process, and invite educators into shared commitments to your child's success.

Key Themes

♦ You are not alone: The special education world involves an array of support services designed to bolster the likelihood of your child's success.

♦ Note-taking is your friend. Write everything down so you can refer back to it later. This chapter includes forms to record key details in an organized fashion.

♦ As a parent, you can help your child identify resources they can tap into when they struggle at school. Learning to self-advocate is key.

♦ The relationship with the case manager is paramount to student success. Get to know your student's case manager well to build a bridge for your child to walk across.

♦ The IEP process involves a series of legally required steps. The chapter will lay each one out for you and help you understand how to make each component most helpful.

♦ Asking the right questions will get you the right answers. This chapter will help you plan for the questions you will ask as a part of the process to learn key information.

♦ Each team member serves a unique purpose. Effective collaboration happens when all participants come together with the same goal: Student success.

You Are Not Alone

I still remember the moment I walked into my house for the first time as a mom. When I left the house, I was an expecting young mother full of hope, excitement, and some trepidation. When I returned, I was a mom. I held a PERSON in my arms. I remember standing in my living room flooded with joy, elation, and sheer panic. Would I be good at this? Would my child thrive? Would I ever get any sleep again? The pressure we can put on ourselves as parents is often unrealistic and unfeasible if we are going to enjoy our lives.

> The pressure we can put on ourselves as parents is often unrealistic and unfeasible if we are going to enjoy our lives.

When your child arrives in special education, you may feel pressure to have all the answers. Perhaps you feel reluctant to ask for help or advocate too much because you do not want to seem like a burden or you wish to appear highly capable. I have definitely suffered from 'supermom' syndrome, trying to do it all. Unfortunately, trying to bring home the bacon and fry it in a pan usually just leaves us fried! The answer? Positive interdependence. A healthy reliance on other people to help accomplish goals together. In this case, the goal is the success of that wonderful little person you are trying to raise into a strong, productive, HAPPY adult.

As you know, special education is focused on teamwork. The IEP is written by a team which includes you, your child, and other professionals as detailed later in this chapter. The plan is implemented by a team. Most special educators are now participants in collaboration as a regular required part of their teaching practice (Friziellie et al., 2016, p. 16). So, what actually makes a team? Is it a collection of people sitting around a table talking? Nope! According to the experts, a "collection of collaborators does not truly become a team until members must rely on one another to accomplish a goal that none could achieve individually" (Dufour et al., 2016, p. 60). This means that every single person involved in the development of the IEP has a critical voice and contribution to make, including YOU!

As you engage in the IEP process, remember that you hold just as much expertise as everyone else around the table. Sure, you may be on their turf and they may have most of the information on the school side of things, but you are the best resource available: An expert on your child. The hope is that all team members come to the table with openness, humility, and active listening at the ready. Any team members who believe they already have 'everything figured out' may struggle to try new ideas and think creatively to best meet your child's needs. If you feel team members are closed off to your ideas, say so! You can let them know using assertive, yet kind, communication (see Chapter 3) to improve the general outcome of the IEP process.

> The hope is that all team members come to the table with openness, humility, and active listening at the ready.

To best understand the team of support available in special education, it may help to understand the legal requirements for IEP meeting participation. The law requires the participation of the student (to the greatest extent possible), the parent/guardian (that's you), the case manager, general education teacher(s), service providers, and an administrator (or administrative designee). Each participant required on the team can offer expertise and helpful information to improve outcomes for students. Table 2.1 details the required members of the IEP team and the expertise they may offer (IRIS Center, 2021).

Activity 6 invites you to identify the team members who will help develop your child's IEP. You may choose to bring this

TABLE 2.1 Required team member in the IEP process and the expertise they offer.

Required Team Member	Expertise They Offer
The student: The student should be included in IEP meetings when appropriate. The school must invite the student when the purpose of an IEP meeting is to discuss post-secondary goals and transition services.	Your child is the most important voice at the table. They possess the fullest knowledge of their own priorities, strengths and needs, preferred accommodations, and both short-term and long-term goals. Your child's voice is the most important throughout this process and they must drive decision-making to foster success.

(Continued)

TABLE 2.1 (*Continued*)

Required Team Member	Expertise They Offer
You! The parent/guardian: A biological parent, foster parent, legal guardian, or an individual who acts in place of the parent (e.g., grandparent, stepparent, or other relatives).	You have so much to offer the team! You can offer meaningful input about priorities, your child's strengths and needs, as well as information about the cultural and developmental appropriateness of the IEP. Your voice is critical to the team.
Special education teacher or special education provider (e.g., related service personnel): An educator with expertise about the disability area and its impact on the student's developmental and educational progress.	The special education teacher brings the team together and orchestrates the 'flow' during the IEP process, guiding suggestions based on knowledge of the special education system and creating an IEP which will best serve the student.
General education teacher: A general educator who is, or will be, a teacher of the child.	The general education teacher has knowledge of the general education curriculum, including the standards and essential learning for each area. The general education teacher also offers a resource to set the stage for successful inclusion.
Administrative designee: A designated representative of the school district, often a special education director or coordinator, or a school principal. Any tenured special educator can serve in this role if the administrator is not available.	This individual is aware of the resources available for the student and how they may access them best. They possess an understanding of school policy and the general education curriculum. Note that the principal attending the meeting is not negative and it does not indicate behavior issues. It's a legal requirement to identify and use resources well.
An educational professional who can interpret the evaluation results (e.g., school psychologist): This role may be filled by any other member on the IEP team, except for a student's parents.	This participant can explain the implications of evaluation results to the team, possessing knowledge of various tools in order to translate data into understandable terms and inform team decisions. They can also offer an understanding of the instructional implications.
Other relevant individuals: Others who have relevant knowledge or expertise regarding the student can be included, such as service providers or advocates. You as a parent can ask for added team members as you wish.	Related services personnel provide specific expertise relevant to student needs (such as physical therapists and speech/language pathologists). Language interpreters have the ability to aid communication between educators and the family when needed. There are multiple advocacy agencies available to support you in understanding the special education process and sharing your voice. A simple Google search can help you find this support in your area.

Team Member Directory

By law, Individual Education Planning teams must include the parent(s) or guardian(s), case manager, general education teacher(s), administrative designee, and any relevant service providers. The student should also be invited as soon as they have the skills to engage in the conversation. The more the student can take the lead, the better! Use this form to keep track of key team members for quick access.

Case Manager:	General Education Teacher(s):
Phone Number/Email Address:	Phone Number/Email Address:
Administrative Designee:	Service Provider:
Phone Number/Email Address:	Phone Number/Email Address:
Service Provider:	Service Provider:
Phone Number/Email Address:	Phone Number/Email Address:

My Network of Resources

Select key areas of your parenting life in which you may benefit from support. Complete this document to save key resources in one place for easy access to help when needs arise. This may include school personnel, advocacy groups, personal mentors, etc.

Area:		
Experts I Know:	**Online Resources:**	**Additional Resources:**

Area:		
Experts I Know:	**Online Resources:**	**Additional Resources:**

Area:		
Experts I Know:	**Online Resources:**	**Additional Resources:**

Who Can Help?

Think about the things you struggle with at school. Use this form to identify adults who can help you when you need it. Also, think about other students who might be there for you during challenges. Then, create a simple plan of action you can take when you face your problem areas during the school day.

Area:		
Adults who can help:	Students who can help:	My Plan:

Area:		
Adults who can help:	Students who can help:	My Plan:

Area:		
Adults who can help:	Students who can help:	My Plan:

along to the meeting and pass it around to easily collect contact information. If you are anything like me, you might find yourself replaying the meeting in your mind at some point later in the day (for me it's often while I'm folding laundry or doing the dishes). You will want to have the contact information on hand so you can ask that brilliant question which comes to you after the meeting. Trust me, special educators do welcome your questions and thoughts so they don't have to go back and make changes later. We love efficiency (we have a lot on our plates)!

Beyond the team of professionals who will develop the IEP, it can also help you to build a network of key support personnel, online resources, and additional resources. Think about the areas in your life in which you need help/information. Maybe this has something to do with your child's medical needs. Perhaps this involves your own self-care and mental health. You can gather these resources in one place through the use of Activity 7, 'My Network of Resources.' Your child may also benefit from identifying key adults, peers, and resources they can turn to in times of difficulty. Activity 8 invites your child to identify 'Who Can Help?' when they need it. This may assist them in solidifying their system of support and finding their voice to self-advocate.

Connecting with the Case Manager

School had always been tough for Darren. He struggled with academics and quickly became frustrated when he didn't seem to 'get it' the way all the other kids 'got it.' He learned early on that he would rather be seen as tough than not-so-smart. He would make sure to get the last laugh whenever there was a conflict. He would push the rules and boundaries set forth by the teachers to the point that the other students wondered if he was the one running the classroom. He put out a gruff, no-nonsense, cool persona of someone who couldn't be ruffled and wouldn't be messed with. It worked for him, at least until he hit middle school.

Suddenly, he went from being the big fish in the little pond of elementary school to being the little fish in the big pond of middle school, and it didn't feel too great. He now had seven classes to impress, seven social groups to conquer, and each of these groups included other big dogs from other schools. His academics continued to flounder, and he found himself lost. His answer? Ramp up his behavior.

In his state of stress about losing face and giving up the 'tough guy' image, he started to lose control of his anger and lash out at other people. Eventually, his parents and teachers had to meet with administrators and start the referral process for special education. By 9th grade, he found himself identified with a learning disability in math, as well as needs in his social/emotional functioning and communication. He would start high school with an individual education plan (IEP) to get through the school day and he would have the support of a case manager, Mr. Washington.

Mr. Washington met Darren on a Monday afternoon. Darren was sick of adults telling him what to do; worn out from not understanding the content and not performing up to grade level standards; and worst of all, he was lonely. His challenges had ended up isolating him from his peers to the point where he didn't have a single social connection left. And now he was irritated that he had to sit down and talk with some guy he didn't even know about stuff he probably didn't care about.

"Darren, I want one thing for you: to figure out who you want to be. It seems like things at school haven't been the best, but school isn't the most important thing to me right now. I just want you to find an easier way of living so you can be happy. It can't be very fun to be in trouble all the time. Are you sick of it?" Mr. Washington asked.

"Yeah, because this school sucks," Darren replied with force.

"If I were in your shoes, I would probably feel the same way," he said. "Here's the thing. You're only in school for a few more years. We're going to work together to help you get through it and get the most out of it so you can be successful.

Most importantly, I want you to figure out who you really are and what makes you happy. I have a whole file of paperwork about how school has been going for you and about all the things you have struggled with. You can read it if you want to. But to me, this file means nothing. This is the past, and it isn't the real you. My job is to help you write a completely new story and ditch the strategies that aren't working for you. So, are you in?"

From that day on, they engaged in frequent conversations about Darren's new identity based on his strengths. Rather than focusing on the areas that presented him with difficulty, Mr. Washington helped him to realize all the good things he brought to the table. Instead of 'covering up' for his academic struggles, he helped him to accept them as surmountable realities of his life. His challenging behaviors quickly dwindled, and he started to build friendships with other students again. Most importantly, Darren realized that he had the power to decide who he wanted to be and how he wanted to act in the world. He didn't need to take on a fake persona to survive at school any longer, and it all came about thanks to the safe and trusting relationship he had with his case manager. So often, all students need is someone at school who believes they can write a new story.

You will find a common theme woven throughout this book: Special education can be seen as a GIFT to your child. This story illustrates the power of the relationship between the student and the case manager. Darren's experience is something I have seen over and over as my amazing colleagues have connected with students, invested in their lives, and helped them create a new story about what school can be. Rarely have I worked with a special educator who got into teaching for fame and fortune. If they did, they would be barking up the

> The case manager/student relationship is a fantastic opportunity for your child to realize the full benefits of special education.

wrong tree. Special educators come to this work to help students thrive. The case manager/student relationship is a fantastic opportunity for your child to realize the full benefits of special education.

What can you typically expect of your child's case manager? Under the umbrella definition of a 'case manager,' one might find many tasks, including assessing students, developing Individual Education Plans, implementing plans, tracking student progress, updating the plan throughout the year, composing progress reports, mentoring students, ensuring adaptations, and supporting student transition into adult life (Bureau of Labor and Statistics, 2021). At the bare minimum, your child's case manager is legally required to orchestrate the development of the IEP, share it with everyone who will implement the plan, and monitor your child's progress to make sure the plan is 'happening' and 'working.'

As a parent, you can encourage your child to connect with their case manager through a variety of strategies. First, refer Chapter 1 for ideas on how you can lead with your child's strengths as you introduce yourself and your child to their case manager. Second, have conversations with your child about this helpful person in their lives and encourage them to reach out for help as needed. Again, we equip our children best when we help them find their own voices of advocacy. Third, you can help foster a positive relationship by getting to know the case manager on a level beyond just a stranger on the other side of the phone or email. See Activity 9 for a form entitled 'Case Manager Information,' which you may share with your child's case manager to invite them to provide information to serve as a jumping-off point for a mutually supportive relationship. As a special education teacher and case manager myself, I use a form similar to this to initiate the connection and students enjoy it. It helps to 'break the ice' and open doors of communication. I also love to share my favorite cheesy joke when I first meet my students: "I may be your case manager, but that doesn't mean I will always be on your case."

Case Manager Information

Greetings! To help our child get to know you, would you please complete this form and return it to us? So excited to build a connection to support a successful school experience. Thank you!

Name:	**Space for a Photo (If you wish)**
Education:	
Hobbies and Fun Facts:	
Contact Information:	
Best time to contact me:	
Favorite tips for success at school:	

Organization and the IEP Process

Okay. Brace yourself. Here comes the information which may be a bit overwhelming! This section will help you develop tools to stay organized throughout the IEP process. Before you even read on, I want you to take a deep breath. Some of you may be experienced with this process so you understand the basics. Some of you may be brand new to the world of special education. Welcome. This process may seem like a LOT at first, but it all unfolds smoothly and honestly, as a parent, you get to do the fun part: Share about your wonderful young person and help develop a plan for school. The 'paperwork' side of things is left to the school personnel, and your task is to sign off on everything at the end.

Before I walk you through the process, please understand that each school and district will have varying practices for how they communicate, plan, and share documents. I am going to offer you a snapshot based on my experience and based on the legal requirements listed under the Individuals with Disabilities Education Improvement Act. This federal law governs the special education process in the United States of America, and all school districts must comply with the core mandates it provides (United States Department of Education, 2004). Your school/district/case manager will have their own style and system. What I share offers you the 'skeleton' so you know what you might expect. Also, note that I will share about the process once your child has already qualified for special education services. Prior to qualifying, the school will have their own process to implement interventions, collect data on effectiveness, engage your child in an evaluation, and gather the results. My best advice during this part of the process would be: Stay flexible, go with the flow, and continuously share about your child's strengths to help guide the team.

> Stay flexible, go with the flow, and continuously share about your child's strengths to help guide the team.

share about your child's strengths to help guide the team. The tools shared in Chapter 1 may be particularly handy during the intervention process.

Once the evaluation results are in, your child will be assigned to a case manager. The case manager will invite you to your very first IEP meeting. The hope is that the team members (listed in Table 2.1) can all attend. It is also important that the school try to work with your schedule and that you try to work with theirs. This can be a bit tricky, but it usually falls into place. If a particular team member is unable to attend, you can excuse them from the meeting. This is at your discretion as a parent. I would HIGHLY recommend that you advocate for a minimum of one general educator, one special educator with expertise in your child's area of need, and one administrative designee around the table. For liability purposes, you should not participate in a one-on-one meeting because there is too much potential for disparities in understanding. When it comes to an IEP meeting, I always feel that 'the more the merrier' is a wise approach.

Now, as a parent coming into a room full of professionals you don't know, you may be thinking, "Yikes" or "Yuck" or "No thanks!" Completely understandable. Here, I remind you that special education can be such a gift to your child and your family. Everyone around the table is there to provide support in one capacity or another. No one is there to judge, criticize, blame, or stir up more problems for you or your child. Although it may be intimidating, remember that your voice is invaluable to the team and that you can trust the process. During the meeting, you will discuss your child's evaluation results and what this means for educational programming. Note that a full evaluation is required every three years, so expect new information according to this timeline. The IEP involves multiple sections which include (PACER Center, 2021):

◆ Present level of educational performance: Discussion of how your child is doing in various areas, including academics, social/emotional/behavioral functioning, cognitive functioning, motor skills, and other areas depending on the evaluation results. Information on the evaluation will fall into this section.

◆ Measurable goals your child will work on. These will include measurable objectives which school personnel will monitor.

- ◆ Student placement: This specifies how much of the student's day will be spent in the special education setting.
- ◆ Special transportation: This notes whether the student will utilize special education transportation.
- ◆ Testing plan: Participation in statewide testing, as well as accommodations such as extended time or tests read aloud.
- ◆ Services: Specific special education services which will take place with the number of minutes and location (general education or special education setting). The service provider is also specified here.
- ◆ Progress reporting frequency and methods. This is required for each term. Note that the IEP meeting serves as one of the progress updates. All other terms will require a written report on how your child is doing.
- ◆ If your child is 14 years old or starting ninth grade, you will discuss transition areas such as jobs/job training, post-secondary education, and community living. The plan will start to prepare your child for a smooth transition into adulthood.

Note that this list isn't in a specific order and that the terminology used may vary from district to district. This is the general outline you can expect. Again, it may seem like a lot to discuss in a short amount of time, but it actually flows well in 'real life.'

As a team, you will draft the plan together. After the meeting, the case manager has ten school days to write the IEP and will send it to you for your approval. You have two calendar weeks to review the plan and ask for any adjustments. Once you sign off, the plan goes into effect for one calendar year. It is of note that the IEP process usually starts well before the end of the IEP year because this allows time to hold the meeting, write the plan, and review the plan. Now, you may feel like this is a lot of information. Activity 10 provides the IEP process in a checklist format so you can see the entire process in a nutshell and mark off the dates each item takes place. Activity 11 provides a note-taking form you may choose to bring along to the meeting in order to keep your own record of the team discussion. Hopefully, these tools help 'boil down' the IEP experience for you and can relieve some of the uncertainty.

IEP Planning Checklist

Each child in special education will participate in school with the use of a legally binding document called an Individual Education Plan (IEP). This checklist walks you through the entire IEP development process from start to finish. You can use this form to record the date of each step in the process for your documentation.

Preparing for the Meeting		
Set up a meeting time.	The case manager will contact you to set up a time which works for the team.	
Receive a written meeting notice.	The case manager will send a written notice which Includes the time, place, purpose and list of attendees.	
Prepare information.	Think about your child's strengths and the needs you hope to address in the meeting.	
Prepare your questions.	Think about the questions you plan to ask and write them down if you choose.	
During the Meeting		
Introductions.	The case manager will introduce team members and have them sign in. You will receive written notice of your procedural safeguards as part of the due process required by law.	
Share key information.	As a team, you will review student eligibility, student strengths, concern areas, assessment results, present levels of performance, progress on prior goals, current priority goals, adaptations and educational services.	
Make key decisions.	As a team, determine answers to key questions such as: Does the placement suit the student? Is it least restrictive? Is there a need for related services, special education transportation, or summer programming? Are the adaptations appropriate?	
After the Meeting		
Review the IEP, ask questions and provide consent.	Within 10 school days of the meeting, the case manager will send the plan for you to review. You can take up to 14 calendar days to review and ask questions. Once you approve, sign to indicate consent and return to the case manager.	
The IEP is shared with all providers.	The case manager will disseminate the plan to stakeholders on a need-to-know basis. All stakeholders are legally required to implement the plan.	
IEP Implementation	The case manager will monitor implementation and serve as the point person on any issues. The plan remains in place for one calendar year. Expect the annual meeting to take place about one month prior to the IEP end date to allow time to create the new IEP for the following year.	

IEP Note-Taking Form

Team Members Present:

General Need-to-Know Information/Current Progress		
Area	**Key Information**	**Plan/Follow-Up Steps**
Goals and Objectives		
Goal Area	**Objectives**	**Who will monitor?**

Accommodations/Modifications/Testing		
Area	Needs	Plan
Accommodations and Modifications In classes		
Accommodations and Modifications For Testing		
Services		

Important Dates:

Meeting Date:

IEP will be sent home (10 school days from meeting date):

IEP will be implemented (14 calendar days after the IEP is sent home for review:

A Focus on Inclusion

One aspect of all team conversations must be a focus on inclusion. This means that your child will be placed in the general education setting to the greatest extent possible in order to meet their needs. The education system as a whole has moved toward a focus on learning for all students, including those identified as having a need for special education services, and thus, teachers have been tasked to create avenues to help all learners succeed in the general education setting. According to research,

> If the ultimate goal of a learning-focused school is to ensure that every student ends each year having acquired the essential skills, knowledge, and behaviors required for success at the next grade level, then all students must have access to grade-level essential curriculum as part of their core instruction.
>
> (Dufour et al., 2016, p. 166)

This means that all classrooms and all teachers have a responsibility to create learning experiences which work for all students. This is great news for students with special education services, because it means that they are more naturally included as a part of the general education classroom along with their peers.

Special education law demands consideration of the Least Restrictive Environment for a student (Heward, 2013), meaning that the team should consider placement in the general education setting first and foremost, and students should only spend time in the special education setting if there is strong information to support this need. As a parent, you can advocate for your child's appropriate placement in the general education setting, with the understanding that some needs simply must be met in a small group environment. The hope is that students with special education services will feel less ostracized or stigmatized as they are a natural part of the general education setting.

In order to promote inclusion, your child's IEP team should focus your child's program on goals which align to grade-level standards, services which take place in the general education setting as much as possible, and adaptations which promote access to the core curriculum (Kirby, 2016). Once an inclusion-oriented IEP is in place, special education teachers can work to ensure that all parts of the plan occur. This involves reminding general education teachers that your child's IEP is a blueprint for their Free and Appropriate Public Education, and it must be implemented as written by the student's team (Yell, 2019; Zirkel, 2017). In a sense, inclusion is not optional, and the details in the plan must unfold as written. As a parent, if you feel that your child is missing out on general education access or that the IEP is not being fully implemented, it may be time to advocate. Chapter 3 will offer you tools to effectively advocate for your child when needed (without exhausting yourself or harming relationships with IEP team members).

No 'Silly' Questions

As a parent, I often feel pressure to know all of the answers. I am an independent person and I like to take care of things on my own. It is not my natural instinct to ask for help when it comes to my children, and I never want to feel like a burden to anyone else. Perhaps you feel the same way. As a special educator and case manager, my message for you is this: PLEASE ask questions. PLEASE ask for help. We don't know what you need or what confuses you unless you ask. The special education world is rife with acronyms, jargon, confusing requirements, etc. This is your official invitation to ask questions, with the understanding that none of them will be viewed as 'silly' and you will not be judged in any way. I promise! In fact, research states that when we ask questions or ask for help, it helps both parties: The asker and the answerer. The answerer has the chance to share their expertise and make a contribution and the asker obtains the information or help they need, ultimately deepening relationships (Nadler, 2015).

> This is your official invitation to ask questions, with the understanding that none of them will be viewed as 'silly' and you will not be judged in any way. I promise!

Just as nobody knows your child better than you, no one knows the special education system better than the educators around the table. They are the experts on the potential services your child may access. As you participate in the special education process, you will discover that asking questions can open doors for your child and help create a plan which makes school 'work' for them. What might this actually look like? The best questions are open-ended in nature to get the team talking about the potential programming options for your child at school. Too often, we fall into the habit of asking 'yes or no' questions which

Crafting Critical Questions

Thinking ahead about the questions you plan to ask during the IEP meeting can help you make best use of the time. Use this form to compose questions you may ask in different areas. Remember, if you don't ask, you won't know!

Area: Social/Emotional/Behavioral Functioning	
Question 1:	Question 2:

Area: Academic Functioning	
Question 1:	Question 2:

Area: Goals/Objectives	
Question 1:	Question 2:

Area: Accommodations and Modifications	
Question 1:	Question 2:

Area: Services	
Question 1:	Question 2:

Area: General Information	
Question 1:	Question 2:

Area: General Information	
Question 1:	Question 2:

fail to elicit discussion. For example, rather than asking 'What are some ideas to help my child manage math class?', we may ask 'Can my child have support in math class?' The second question narrows the potential responses and may limit the answers received.

We are wise to craft questions which invite elaborative responses. I call these 'invitational' questions. Two helpful stems which lead to open communication include 'What are some…' and 'How might…' For example, you may ask, 'What are some possibilities for accommodations?' or 'How might we best help my child with managing their emotions at school?' Activity 12 offers an activity entitled 'Crafting Invitational Questions' which offers you the chance to develop open-ended questions which may help open the lines of communication with your child's IEP team.

Shared Commitments = Shared Success

The act of parenting can be loaded with emotion in that it is one of the most personal and emotionally taxing endeavors an individual may experience. As a parent, you bring your own perspectives and experiences to the way you interact with your child and with the school system. We all have our own perspectives on school and education. Some of us liked school and enjoyed our time as students, and thus, it's easy for us to pass along a love for school. Conversely, if you are anything like me, you didn't like school much and had a hard time. This message is something we may inadvertently share with our children. I struggled to sit still and listen for hours and hours during my educational experiences, and my son happens to struggle with the same issue. As a mom, I must intentionally choose my messages to him in order to support his educational success. I can empathize with his struggles while encouraging him to engage in learning in the way that his teachers expect.

Our children are constantly learning from us. They watch what we say and do very carefully, and pick up on the nuances in our belief systems. If we convey frustration and disdain for school, they may mirror this to their detriment in the educational

> You can help your child by talking about school in a positive way as much as possible. You can also support their success by emphasizing the importance of education.

environment. If we convey excitement about school and learning, they may follow suit. Please know that school is a place for every single child, and that educators want to meet your child's needs. You can help your child by talking about school in a positive way as much as possible. You can also support their success by emphasizing the importance of education, even if this isn't necessarily a message you received growing up. Finally, you can help your child to understand that special education can be a gift to their learning. They have the benefit of a team of support (I like to call them coaches and cheerleaders) to surround them and bolster their success.

Articulating shared commitments can help set the stage for effective collaboration between students, parents, and special education teachers. Activity 13 offers an example of a document entitled 'Shared Commitments' which your child's team may use to articulate the roles and responsibilities of each participant. Offering this document serves to build trust and may stave off difficulty before it occurs. Taking the time to review this document may create a powerful avenue for healthy collaboration throughout the school year. You may also choose to create your own version of this 'shared commitments' document so that you can tailor it to the specific needs of all participants.

The shared commitment document may be particularly helpful to the IEP team. The IEP process is a wonderful opportunity to talk about everyone's shared investment in your child's success. At a minimum, it may be helpful to have a conversation about the ideas listed on the document even if there isn't time to go through it and compile signatures. The idea is that everyone agrees to a series of simple premises which include: School is important and will take a priority. All team members are here to help make school a success. The shared goal all team members hold is to help the child meet theirs.

> The IEP process is a wonderful opportunity to talk about everyone's shared investment in your child's success.

ACTIVITY THIRTEEN

Shared Commitments

Student Commitments:

- I will come to school every day well rested and on time and remain in school until dismissal.
- I will come to school with necessary materials and prepared to work.
- I will complete all assignments on time.
- I will ask for help or assignments missed when needed.
- I will respect the rights of others at all times.

Parent/Guardian Commitments:

- I will make sure my child is well rested and at school on time and remains in school until dismissal.
- I will make sure my child is prepared with the necessary materials and ready to learn.
- I will communicate any concerns with my child's case manager and/or teacher.
- I will read, sign, and return progress reports and teacher communications and attend conferences/meetings as requested.

Teacher Commitments:

- I will ensure that the Individual Education Plan takes place.
- I will provide a classroom environment conducive to learning.
- I will communicate my expectations, instructional goals, and grading system with parents through conferences, progress reports, e-mails, or by telephone.
- I will provide students who have been absent with missed assignments.
- I will accept and respect the cultural differences of my students.
- I will do whatever it takes to see students make progress on their goals.
- I will respond to requests thoroughly and as soon as possible.

Signatures:

Student: _____

Parents: _____

Teacher: _____

Conclusion

The special education process can seem overwhelming and cumbersome, but it doesn't have to be. You can view this as an opportunity for your child to receive the necessary support to make school a better experience. This is a gift to you and your family. As you move through each stage in the process, you can use the activities in this chapter to keep track of key team members and to build your network of resources. You are not alone in this, and no one expects you to have all the answers. Help your child identify resources for assistance when needed, and you will find that they grow in their ability to self-advocate. One of the most important bridges you will build is the relationship with the case manager. Learn about this educator and connect as much as you can to leverage the special education process for your child.

Remember that everyone around the IEP table shares the same goal: To follow the legally required special education process in order to improve positive outcomes for your learner. The tools in this chapter can walk you through the paperwork side of things and help you take notes on team discussions. Prepare and ask questions early and often to obtain the information you need. Finally, commit to making school a positive experience for your child by highlighting the positive aspects of the educational experience. Even if you feel frustrated or weighed down by the education system at times, try to share positive information with your child to encourage them to thrive in the school setting. All members of the IEP team can come together through the development of shared commitments to the child's success.

Chapter 2 Simple Snapshot

♦ Keep track of team members and their contact information for easy connection when you need it. Follow-up questions are welcome after IEP meetings.

- ◆ Build and utilize a network of resources such as school personnel, websites, support organizations, and even other parents to help you find the information you need.
- ◆ Encourage your child to ask for help at school and make sure they know the members of their special education team.
- ◆ Remember that the IEP is a legally binding document and that you have the final say in approving it. It's okay to ask for tweaks, revisions, or additions. Keep these within reason with the understanding that case managers are busy and often overloaded.
- ◆ Take careful notes in IEP meetings and never engage in a meeting one-on-one in order to prevent issues with liability or confusion about what was shared. The more the merrier!
- ◆ Ask questions which are open-ended in nature to get team members talking. Remember that there are no 'silly' questions and that educators are happy to help.
- ◆ Invite all team members into shared commitments to supporting your child. Help your child commit to making school an important priority and to doing their best.

Chapter 2 Reflection Questions

Use the following questions to reflect on what you have learned in the chapter. You may choose to journal about them or discuss them with a friend or book club.

1. What is your experience with the special education system so far? What has gone well for you in this process?
2. What are some challenges you have experienced with the special education process thus far and how might the content of this chapter help you navigate them?
3. In your own words, what is the role of your child's case manager? What are your thoughts on the development of this relationship?

4. When you think about the IEP process, what jumps out at you? Which areas will be most hopeful and which concern you most?
5. What is your style when it comes to asking questions? Do you like to be independent or are you open to asking for help? How might the tools in this chapter help you seek out the answers you need?
6. What are some of the commitments you hope to share with your child and the school? What do you expect of your child when it comes to education? What do you expect of school personnel?

References

Bureau of Labor and Statistics. (2021). *Occupational outlook handbook: Special education teachers*. U.S. Bureau of Labor and Statistics https://www.bls.gov/ooh/education-training-and-library/special-education-teachers.htm#tab-6.

DuFour, R., DuFour, R., Eaker, R., Many, T.W., & Mattos, M. (2016). *Learning by doing*. Bloomington, IN: Solution Tree Press.

Friziellie, H., Schmidt, J., & Spiller, J. (2016). *Yes we can! General and special educators collaborating in a professional learning community*. Bloomington, IN: Solution Tree Press.

Heward, W.L. (2013). *Six major principles of IDEA*. Metro State Faculty Resources. http://faculty.metrostate.edu/barrerma/Fall2015/Six%20Major%20Principles%20of%20IDEA.pdf.

Kirby, M. (2016). Implicit assumptions in special education policy: Promoting full inclusion for students with learning disabilities. *Child & Youth Care Forum*, vol. 46, no. 2, pp. 175–191, doi:10.1007/s10566-016-9382-x.

Nadler, A. The other side of helping: Seeking and receiving help." *The Oxford Handbook of Prosocial Behavior*, vol. 1. Oxford University Press, 2015, doi:10.1093/oxfordhb/9780195399813.013.004.

PACER Center. (2021). *Overview of the special education process*. Pacer.org https://www.pacer.org/parent/understanding-the-spec-ed-process.asp.

The IRIS Center. (2021). IEP team members. *Vanderbilt University*. https://iris.peabody.vanderbilt.edu/wp-content/uploads/modules/iep01/pdf/IEP_Team_Members.pdf#content.

United States Department of Education. (2004). *Individuals with disabilities education improvement act, 20 U.S.C. § 1400*. https://sites.ed.gov/idea/statute-chapter-33/subchapter-i/1400.

Yell, M.L. (2019). *The law and special education* (5th ed.). London, England: Pearson Education.

Zirkel, P.A. (2017). Failure to implement the IEP: The third dimension of FAPE under IDEA. *Journal of Disability Policy Studies*, vol. 28, no. 3, pp. 174–179, doi:10/1177/1044207317732582.

3

Communication and Advocacy Tools

Mr. Bradford decided to attend the parent teacher organization (PTO) meeting to have a voice in his school. As a passionate young father, he had a lot to say about issues in the school and the direction it should be going. He planned to be a warrior for systemic change in this antiquated institution. The PTO meeting would be one place to make his valuable voice heard.

The meeting began, and the principal introduced Mr. Bradford as the new member of the group. He was warmly welcomed. The principal then opened the floor for committee members to share ideas for school improvements this year.

"I would like to start a sub-committee called the 'hallway beautification committee' to make the space more pleasant for our children," said a woman named Ms. Peretti. "I am actually an interior designer and would love to help make the space more inviting for our children. Right now it's a little… clinical."

Mr. Bradford was appalled! What a shallow, superficial concern. In one statement, Ms. Peretti had summed up everything that was wrong with education! He had to speak up.

"Ma'am, no disrespect, but who cares about what the hallways look like when we have children who aren't showing growth in their academic skills! This is a school, not one of your design projects. It's for learning, right? You want to waste everyone's time with a hallway beautification committee? That's embarrassing, to be honest. I mean WOW. Ridiculous. Honestly, you probably shouldn't even be on this committee."

Silence. An awkward sniffle from Ms. Peretti. She didn't say a word for the rest of the meeting and stared with great interest into her lap. No one else spoke either. It was as if the oxygen had been sucked out of the room. Finally, the principal spoke.

DOI: 10.4324/9781003364443-5

"Okay, everyone, let's move on and I will send out an email about Ms. Peretti's idea. I think it would be great to improve the look of our hallways, so thank you," said the principal. "Let's take a look at the next item on the agenda," Everyone shifted in their chairs. For the remainder of the meeting, very few people spoke up besides Mr. Bradford. He provided a robust opinion on every agenda item. At the end of the meeting, the principal stopped him on his way out the door.

"I really appreciate your input, Mr. Bradford, but I'd also love to hear from other parents as well. Maybe at our next meeting you could go a little easy on the rest of the team? To be honest, during your first few meetings on any new committee, it's probably a good idea to do more listening than talking so you can get to know everyone in the group."

"Oh yes, sure... No problem at all," Mr. Bradford stammered as he fumbled in his pocket for his keys and headed out the door.

Driving home, a sudden wave of self-awareness flooded Mr. Bradford. He realized he had been too harsh, he had hurt Ms. Peretti's feelings and derailed the meeting in one statement. Mr. Bradford was completely humbled. He later sent an email in which he apologized profusely to the principal and Ms. Peretti. He learned that even when he felt impassioned and needed to speak up, he needed to do so with care, kindness, and empathy in order for his message to be heard. This would not only help his own success in advocacy, it would help his child as well.

When you discover an unmet need in the 'school life' of your child, it is time for wise advocacy.

Mr. Bradford did the right thing. He spoke up for his child. The trouble is, he did the right thing in the wrong way. As a parent, there will be moments in which you need to advocate for your child's needs. As we've stated throughout this book, you know your child best, and thus, you need to inform the school and Individual Education Planning (IEP) team at times. Through the use of wise and strategic practices, we can best meet this challenge with little stress while preserving positive relationships. Put simply, advocacy is the act or process of supporting a cause or proposal (Merriam-Webster, 2021). When you discover an unmet need in the 'school life' of your child, it is time for wise advocacy. If you feel that steps are needed to ensure that the IEP is fully implemented, this can also involve an advocacy conversation regarding your child. This chapter will explore the advocacy process and provide tools and strategies to help create less stress and more results when it is time to speak up.

Key Themes

◆ There is no rush! Taking a moment to pause and think before speaking up can make a world of difference in advocacy conversations.

◆ Assume positive intent: Make the decision to assume that all school professionals want what's best for your child and they are doing their best.

◆ Venting to other parents, or even to your child, may be tempting, but it actually gives more energy to the problem rather than the solution.

◆ Using active listening in advocacy conversations can help reduce negative emotions and ensure effective communication.

◆ Being proactive rather than reactive can help you to solve problems before they start and reduce the need for advocacy conversations.

◆ Using assertive, clear communication which isn't too passive or too assertive can help ensure that your message is heard.

◆ The best advocate for your child is your child! Helping them focus on their bright future can help you set the stage for growth in their self-advocacy abilities.

◆ Take time to reflect on various situations in order to determine whether the best course of action is to accept what is happening or advocate for change.

The Power of a Pause

I'm a fast thinker, talker, and replier. I have a lot to say, and I tend to react impulsively at times. Thankfully, I have a seasoned colleague who shares a simple bit of advice which has become a bit of a mantra for me: "Slow down, Sunshine." I cannot tell you how many times I have wanted to unsend an email or un-speak something I have said in a meeting because I spoke or replied too soon. This isn't necessarily the worst thing, because it shows that I am passionate. We all love our children, and at times, you will find that the 'mama bear' or 'papa bear' within you wakes up when you perceive a threat. The only trouble is, at times, we say things which come out too harshly and emotionally, and the next thing you know, we have created conflict. So, I offer you the most beautiful piece of advice I may have to give in this book with regard to connecting with school personnel:

PAUSE.
STOP.
AND THINK BEFORE YOU SPEAK.
So simple. So beautiful. So difficult.

The moment we become parents, we begin to compile our own unwritten handbook on how to take good care of our children. Many of us arrive at well-rooted philosophies of parenting and we hold to these passionately. We love our children and we love our point of view about them. There are so many different ways to approach all situations in education, we are bound to have conflicting views and opinions with school practices at times. No matter how 'right' you think you are, it serves you well to take a moment and consider alternative perspectives. It can be so powerful to take a moment to organize your thinking and figure out the best way to frame your point so that it won't create a rift. Try to remove emotions from the picture because they just tend to charge things up. Our big feelings can be our worst enemies at times when we are trying to collaborate and communicate.

> No matter how 'right' you think you are, it serves you well to take a moment and consider alternative perspectives.

Too often, the need to advocate for your child elicits an immediate response or a 'knee-jerk' reaction. This is completely natural and to be expected. You have every right to say and think and feel whatever you want as the parent in the situation. The only trouble is, the impulsive response isn't the most thoughtful or diplomatic, which can lead to sticky situations and even burned bridges. Next thing you know, that was the exact bridge your child needed to walk across. I promise you that you will save yourself from negative consequences and stress when you stop to pause before reacting. This offers you the opportunity to check in with your emotions, identify the true issue, and take wise steps toward solutions.

Assume Positive Intent

As we discussed in-depth in Chapter 2, the IEP process is collaborative in nature. The legal requirements mandate that there are many voices around the table. One premise which can be very helpful in any 'teamwork' situation is the commitment to 'assume positive intent.' This means that we choose to trust that school personnel and other stakeholders want to do what is best, and they are operating from a well-meaning place. This can completely transform relationships for the better. In human relationships, beliefs about others have a causal impact on their attitudes, actions, and performance, and simply assuming positive intent can change the way colleagues respond to each other (Crandall and Kincaid, 2017). Parents and IEP team members who assume positive intent are better able to connect in difficult situations and consider various angles to potentially solve problems. This bolsters creativity, problem-solving potential and can lead to improved results for your child.

> It helps so much to CHOOSE the mindset that all people, students, colleagues, administrators, etc., are doing the best they can with the tools and beliefs they have.

It helps so much to CHOOSE the mindset that all people, students, colleagues, administrators, etc., are doing the best they can with the tools and beliefs they have. Assuming positive intent demands empathy as all communicators strive to see situations from the other person's point of view. The term empathy applies to both mental and emotional states: Cognitive empathy involves the capacity to represent other people's thoughts, beliefs, and intentions; emotional empathy is defined as experiencing what it feels like for another person to experience a certain state of emotion (Yirmiya and Siedman, 2021). When assuming positive intent, we can imagine that the other person is operating from a shared commitment to your child's learning and positive outcomes. Making a commitment to assume positive intent from other team members may not always be easy, but it can help you stay more positive through the advocacy process.

I have something to confess. I am not a naturally angry person and I don't get upset easily. If I did, I couldn't serve students as a special education teacher. I can roll with the punches and go with the flow, keeping my eyes focused on the positive. Except when it comes to one thing: My children. I am fiercely protective when it comes to my kids, and if I feel they have been wronged in any way, I can quickly become upset. This is true of many parents. We love our children dearly, we want what's best for them, and in many ways, we are biologically programmed to protect those within the scope of our parenting (whether we are their biological parents or not). When upset, one of my habits is to find another mom friend or my significant other and start spouting off about my anger and frustrations.

You may have heard terms such as 'decompressing' or 'venting' referring to conversations about negative situations. In the past, I have vented more than a fireplace flue in winter when I am upset, particularly when it comes to my children. There is a common conception in education that 'venting' is a necessary part of life in order to reduce stress and maintain sanity. While it may feel good to express negative emotions such as anger, sadness, or fear, discussing these emotions may actually serve to make you feel worse, especially if you don't find a way to gain a positive alternative perspective. There is certainly some value in processing situations in order to find proactive solutions. However, venting in the wrong contexts can create many issues and can actually give more fuel to the negativity fire. I find that 'venting' feels like complaining and wallowing in the muck for me. I have learned to avoid these conversations and let go of the bad by intentionally shifting my mind back to all that is good after a tough situation or when I am feeling upset.

> There is certainly some value in processing situations in order to find proactive solutions. However, venting in the wrong contexts can create many issues and can actually give more fuel to the negativity fire.

Research shows that venting is a behavior that seems to make individuals feel better, but in actuality, venting rewards and reinforces negative beliefs that might not even be true, deepening the frustration a person already felt (Supiano, 2021). Thus, the idea that you need to vent in order to manage stress works against your ultimate goal: moving on and feeling better. Yes, you need safe and trusting relationships in which you can be honest and express yourself. However, you are wise to sustain your commitment to a focus on the positive as much as possible. Sharing about the negative emotions may actually cause you to re-experience the pain, increasing the experience of anger, grief, or anxiety associated with the difficult incident (Suttie, 2021). Not the goal!

There is an alternative! You do indeed need support at times and I suggest that you enlist a trusted friend or partner as a 'solution partner,' as opposed to a 'venting buddy.' The hope is that this person becomes a trusted confidant and source of positive support. I believe that building friendships and developing a support network helps parents of children with special needs sustain their happiness. Isolation is a one-way ticket to increased stress, and a problem shared is a problem cut in half. The focus of a 'solution partner' relationship is to discover strategies to solve problems rather than complain about them. The right relationship with a positive and uplifting person can sustain your heart and help you focus on solutions rather than adding energy to the problem. Table 3.1 differentiates a 'venting buddy' vs. a 'solution partner.'

TABLE 3.1 Distinctions between a 'venting buddy' and a 'solution partner.'

Venting Buddy Behaviors	Solution Partner Behaviors
Shares in complaining.	Focuses on potential positive aspects in the situation or new learnings which may come from the problem.
Dwells in negative emotions.	Seeks to listen and offer a safe space for emotional expression while guiding the speaker toward the positive.
'Feeds the fire' by offering additional negative information.	Waits and listens before offering perspectives and advice. When they do offer information, it is focused on the good, the helpful, and the kind perspective.
Expresses sympathy or pity, feeling bad for the person sharing.	Expresses empathy by sharing the difficulty with the person in order to offer true support and help move them out of their negative emotions.
Offers negative stories about similar situations they have experienced.	Offers positive information regarding their knowledge and experience with the issue in order to help, not deepen the difficulty.
Agrees that the problem is a significant difficulty and even makes it seem worse.	Validates the person's feelings while helping them to regain perspective and realize that the problem may not be as bad as it seems. 'This too shall pass.' thinking.

Active Listening Skills

The first thing to go out the window when I go into 'mama bear' mode is my listening skills. I go on the defensive. I just want to talk and it doesn't matter what anyone is saying. This works to the detriment of problem-solving and advocacy. Often, miscommunication is the root of most interpersonal problems, and active listening is the only way to rebuild understanding after there is a disconnect. Active listening is often an overlooked skill which requires individuals to truly put aside their own judgments and become intent on what the speaker has to say, demanding openness to the ideas of others (McAdamis, 2013). Listening to each other is key in any collaborative relationship, and it sets the stage for empathy as team members share their perspectives. We can't fully and fairly consider the viewpoints of others unless we listen to what they have to share.

> Listening to each other is key in any collaborative relationship and it sets the stage for empathy as team members share their perspectives.

There are numerous barriers to active listening which can stand in the way of effective communication. Selective listening, interrupting, contradicting, and judging are common barriers which arise in countless human interactions every day (Desai, 2018). Rather than hearing only what we want to hear, we can carefully listen for the true messages. Instead of cutting off a communicator with our own thoughts and assertions, we can wait, pause, and focus on the speaker's words. Too often, we are busy planning our reply while the other person is speaking, causing us to miscommunicate and leading to problems. Contradicting and judging can be natural reactions when you hear something you don't agree with. Here again, the power of the pause comes into play. It is completely acceptable to disagree with what someone is saying, but first, make sure you hear and receive the full message before drawing your conclusions.

As mentioned in Chapter 2, the IEP process includes an annual meeting in which active listening can greatly support your participation and understanding. After hearing individuals share, you may verbally review information provided by the speaker, highlight key themes, and write down key information (Da Fonte and Barton-Arwood, 2017). Another tool of active listening during the meeting is an open mind. The hope is that all participants come to the planning meeting ready to truly hear what others have to share and to make planning decisions accordingly. While it is certainly acceptable to hold fast to one's own perspective, an open mind may be your best ally in the collaboration process. Perspective taking, or a willingness to consider matters from the other person's point of view, is a commitment healthy teams may make to improve collaboration, and this definitely applies to the IEP team (Dufour et al., 2016). If you don't feel that you are being heard at the planning meeting, or if you feel other voices are being stifled, you have every right to express this with kindness and assertiveness.

> The hope is that all participants come to the planning meeting ready to truly hear what others have to share and to make planning decisions accordingly.

It is also helpful for teachers to adopt a mindful approach to listening as you engage in advocacy conversations and IEP meetings. Through this approach, the listener stays in the present moment and sets aside their own busy thoughts, opinions, and stressors. When you need to participate in any conversation with school personnel, particularly those which may be difficult, focus your energy on the positive outcome you desire, take a deep breath, clear other clutter out of your mind, and actively take in the other person's message (Cayoun et al., 2018). Mindfulness allows a listener to clear away cognitive clutter and offer their entire, present self to the speaker (Kabat-Zinn, 2016). The result may be better communication and less stress for communicators on both sides of the conversation. Mindful listening decreases the likelihood that key messages will be misinterpreted, leading to potential problems and confusion. So relax, focus on the positive, open your mind, and listen deeply to what others have to share. It will benefit your child in the long run!

Proactive vs. Reactive

So many problems we face in special education are preventable. However, we too often find ourselves in survival mode reacting to negative situations after they have already occurred. One of the greatest gifts experience has given me as a special education teacher is the ability to recognize common patterns among my students and colleagues. I can assure you that the month of September tends to involve a bit of a honeymoon period. I can assure you that the month of February is when the school year begins to feel long and there is a dip in student moods. I can almost promise you that as the end of the school year nears in May, student energy levels tend to rise and focus tends to dwindle. Recognizing the potential issues presented by these patterns can help me be proactive. I can expect changes in student moods in February and work more fun and enjoyment into my lessons. I can expect heightened energy levels in May and work in more calming activities to help students regain their focus as much as possible.

As a parent, you know many of the common patterns of action demonstrated by your child. Sharing these with the school can help the team to be proactive and solve problems before they start.

Recognizing and responding to patterns is one way to be proactive. As a parent, you know many of the common patterns of action demonstrated by your child. Sharing these with the school can help the team to be proactive and solve problems before they start. In order to be proactive, consider the outcomes you hope for your child and the obstacles which may stand in your child's way. Communicate these potential issues with your child's IEP team and brainstorm solutions together to set the stage for success. Note that this does not mean a narrow focus on the negative. Rather, the hope is that team members will have necessary information to create a safe and supportive environment for your child. Teacher Tool 14, 'Solving Problems Before They Start,' may help you identify problems before they occur and plan for the necessary steps school personnel may take to set the stage for better outcomes for your child (Activity 14).

Solving Problems Before They Start

Consider situations in which you may need to advocate for your child. How might you solve potential problems before they start? Complete this form to identify specific proactive actions you may take to set the stage for success.

Potential Issue:			
Who could help?	What may be needed?	What will I communicate?	How might this help?

Potential Issue:			
Who could help?	What may be needed?	What will I communicate?	How might this help?

Potential Issue:			
Who could help?	What may be needed?	What will I communicate?	How might this help?

Assertive, Yet Kind

For many years, I taught social skills groups for students in middle school with special education services in the area of emotional/behavioral disorder. I should mention that I really dislike that label and I don't think it serves students well. In these groups, there was a huge focus placed on communication skills. In my experience, nearly all conflicts students experienced could be traced back to a problem with communication. At times, they misunderstood a teacher's directions and this was viewed as disrespect. In other situations, they shared an opinion with too much aggression, leading to escalated conflicts with peers.

> In my experience, nearly all conflicts students experienced could be traced back to a problem with communication.

In my special education practice, I have found that a focus on communication skills can improve outcomes in almost all other areas of education. School is a constant exercise for students in the areas of reading, writing, speaking, and listening. These four abilities can make or break their success. The same goes for teams of professionals. The stronger we can communicate, particularly in speaking and listening, the better we can come together to meet student needs.

In human interaction, the most effective and helpful form of verbal communication is assertiveness. Assertiveness is a form of communication involving a confident statement which expresses a point of view without aggressively threatening the rights of another or submissively permitting another to ignore or deny one's rights or point of view (Cayoun et al., 2018). Consider the common tale of Goldilocks and the Three Bears. In this classic story, Goldilocks finds herself tasting porridge, which is too cold, too hot, and then 'just right.' The same can be said of communication. Overly aggressive communication could be seen as 'too hot,' alienating others and standing in the way of the message. Passive communication could be seen as 'too cold,' causing the individual to shy away and fail to convey their message at all. As a teacher, I have found that students respond best to assertive communication, and as a parent, the same holds true in my conversations with school personnel.

I assure you that if you develop the habits of assertive communication, you will garner respect from school personnel and you will be a stronger collaborator. Say what needs to be said to the right person with as much kindness and diplomacy as possible. You will feel better when you get your message out rather than bottling it up. Your messages will be better received when you take care not to be too aggressive. An assertive communication style may be 'just right' to help you sustain positive relationships and secure the resources your child needs.

> All of us can cultivate our 'assertiveness muscle' and move toward a more centered, effective approach to communication.

The beautiful thing about humanity is that we are all so incredibly unique. Some of us are hard-wired to be more aggressive. Our first reaction is anger and we often act accordingly. Think about that friend who can't stand a traffic jam and tends toward frustration with other drivers. Some of us tend toward passiveness. The last thing on earth this person wants is to make any waves or to upset the status quo. Both types of people are necessary and helpful in this world. We need all parts of the puzzle to make up our wonderful human experience. The trouble is, when either style moves to the extreme, it harms relationships and creates an inability to work together. All of us can cultivate our 'assertiveness muscle' and move toward a more centered, effective approach to communication.

You may cultivate your assertive communication style by engaging in self-reflection on your current tendencies with regard to interaction. Teacher Tool 23, "My Communication Style," offers a reflection you may complete to identify your current communication tendencies and move toward assertiveness. This activity also involves scenarios which can help you imagine how you might respond in a passive, aggressive, or assertive way. Preference on assertiveness will serve you well in future communication (Activity 15).

One of the easiest ways to ensure your statements are assertive in nature is to favor 'I statements' rather than 'You statements.'

My Communication Style

Complete this activity to reflect on your communication style and evaluate various scenarios to identify response options. Keep in mind that an assertive communication style may support your ability to be heard and to best collaborate with school personnel.

Describe situations which bring out the three types of communication styles in you. When are you most Passive? Aggressive? Assertive?		
Passive:	Aggressive:	Assertive:

Consider this scenario: You are having trouble getting in touch with your child's case manager and have left multiple phone messages and sent numerous emails. When they finally call you back, you are irritated. Describe the passive, aggressive and assertive response:		
Passive:	Aggressive:	Assertive:

Consider this scenario: Your child reports that a teacher allowed another child to get away with bullying them during class and you feel upset.		
Passive:	Aggressive:	Assertive:

Consider this scenario: During your child's IEP meeting, a teacher is speaking very negatively and you get the sense that they aren't giving your child a fair chance at success due to past mistakes.		
Passive:	Aggressive:	Assertive:

Final Reflection: What tools or ideas might help you to cultivate assertiveness?

'I Statements'

Help prepare your child to engage in self advocacy using 'I Statements.' Read each situation together. Write an 'I Statement' to address each scenario. Remember that the formula for an 'I Statement' is:

"I feel _____ when you _____. Could you please _____."

Someone keeps saying mean things to you at lunch.		
I FEEL:	WHEN YOU:	COULD YOU PLEASE:

A friend tells you that your shirt is ugly.		
I FEEL:	WHEN YOU:	COULD YOU PLEASE:

Your teacher asks you to do a math problem and you don't know how to do it.		
I FEEL:	WHEN YOU:	COULD YOU PLEASE:

Another student steps on your toes in line and it doesn't seem like an accident.		
I FEEL:	WHEN YOU:	COULD YOU PLEASE:

You see someone picking on one of your friends.		
I FEEL:	WHEN YOU:	COULD YOU PLEASE:

An 'I statement' shares your perspective from your first-person understanding. In contrast, a 'you statement' shares what you think another person is doing, which can be seen as blaming or accusatory. You and your child can both benefit from the regular use of assertive communication, and 'I statements' offer a simple starting point to practice. You can help your child advocate for themself by encouraging 'I statements,' rather than 'you statements,' as a regular part of communication at home. This can even help reduce conflict with other family members or siblings. How nice does that sound? In all conversations, including those involving advocacy, using 'I Statements' may help communicators share their perspectives without causing others to feel attacked or upset. Activity 16, 'I Statements,' may be used with your child to help them practice the ability to assert themselves most effectively. You may also benefit from using 'I Statements' when communicating your perspectives with assertiveness.

> An 'I statement' shares your perspective from your first-person understanding. In contrast, a 'you statement' shares what you think another person is doing, which can be seen as blaming or accusatory.

Dear Future Me

The most powerful and capable advocate for your child is the person they will always have with them, no matter what happens: Themself. You will not always be there, their case manager will not always be there, their teacher won't always be there. No matter where your child falls on the spectrum of communication skills, it is important to cultivate self-advocacy as much as possible. The best way to enlist your child in speaking up for their own needs? Help them CARE DEEPLY about their own success and their future. Apathy is a natural human tendency, and it can be even more apparent for children with special needs because they come to depend on adults in their lives. Why complete a task for myself when an adult will come along and speak for me or complete the task for me? As a teacher, I am constantly holding myself back so that my students can find their own voices, complete tasks on their own, and tap into ownership for their own lives. It's a beautiful thing to see them accomplish tasks with independence when in the past, they would have waited for an adult to complete it for them.

The fancy word for what we are discussing here is self-determination. The term 'self-determination' refers to a combination of knowledge, beliefs, and skills that enable a person to engage in self-regulated, goal-directed behavior with autonomy, taking control of their own destiny (Lopez et al., 2020). Essentially, children who experience self-determination can make decisions regarding their lives and take action to carry out these plans. A series of skills combine to create self-determination within children. These include attitudes and abilities such as self-awareness, assertiveness, creativity, pride in oneself, problem-solving, and self-advocacy skills (National Parent Center on Transition and Employment, 2019). It can certainly be scary to let our children 'take the wheel' and make their own decisions, and indeed, sometimes, they will make mistakes, but we prepare them to be successful self-advocates when we let go and let them soar. This is definitely easier said than done, especially when there are concerns about vulnerability related to the disability area. I can assure you, it's so worth it!

As you hope to set the stage for future success in the life of your child, you are a key player to help them successfully accomplish the challenge of transition throughout their educational lives. Moving from kindergarten to first grade? Transition. Moving from elementary school to middle school? Transition. Finding the right path after high school? Transition. Times of transition can be scary and intimidating for children (and their grown-ups), and I have seen it bring out some pretty tough behavioral responses. However, the presence of a loving, caring team can make all the difference. Here, we arrive at another aspect of special education I absolutely love, the chance to be that supportive presence as students navigate transitions. As a parent, you can help support your child through this process by encouraging them to dream, learn, and gain independence.

One key ingredient in self-determination and self-advocacy is CONFIDENCE! Cultivating confidence can help the child to realize success after transitioning from one setting to another. When a child prepares for a transition and succeeds, they grow in their self-determination skills and their belief in their own capacity. Success begets success, so we serve our children best when we find avenues for them to be successful in any small ways. Children grow in motivation and feel inspired to continue on their path toward a positive adult life. Too often, they have received negative messages about their own potential and they need the chance to break through the limiting beliefs they have held in the past.

What is the goal of all of our efforts in special education and parenting alike? I believe that from the very first day of school, from the very first interaction with a teacher, the goal is to start building the skills and abilities necessary for the student to manage adult life on the other end of their education. Special education is the perfect place for this to take place because we get to tailor our efforts to the precise needs of the student. We have the opportunity to see incredible outcomes when we serve as advocates who fully leverage the resources available to meet student needs.

> From the very first day of school, from the very first interaction with a teacher, the goal is to start building the skills and abilities necessary for the student to manage adult life on the other end of their education.

One strategy you may employ to help your child own their future and engage in self-encouragement is to invite them to write a letter to themselves. The idea is to help your child to recognize what is going well and to believe in the potential they hold for a bright future. When students compose a positive letter to themselves, there are two moments of benefit: First, when they engage in reflection by writing the letter, and second, when they receive the letter later in the school year or later in life (Vogelsinger, 2016). Activity 17 offers an exercise entitled 'Dear Future Self' which asks your child to compose a letter to themself to engage in positive thinking about the future. You can also write a letter to your future child which follows a similar structure. Save your letter or letters as a 'time capsule' of sorts to read

Dear Future Me

Write a letter of encouragement to yourself. Then, take all the steps you need to get yourself there. Don't be afraid to ask for help!

Dear Future Me,   Date: _____

Today, I am _____ years old. I am in _____ grade.

Some things I am good at are _____

_____

My favorite things to do are _____

_____

Some things I have learned are _____

_____

I am working on _____

_____

I believe that I can _____

_____

In 10 years I hope that I am _____

_____

Sincerely,

Your Name: _____

Note: Invite your child to compose this letter, save it, and then share it later in life!

together at a later date, such as a transition milestone. You may also share this activity with your child's case manager or teacher as a fun activity for your child and classmates.

Accept or Advocate?

One of my favorite children's books and Disney films is 'Winnie the Pooh' by A.A. Milne (1954). In fact, I have heard it said that the characters in this work represent different categories of difficulty our students in special education may experience. Pooh struggles with his cognitive abilities; Rabbit has challenges with anxiety; Tigger has a touch of attention deficit hyperactivity disorder; Piglet has a speech fluency issue; and finally, we can't forget our dear Eeyore who is a pessimist who could probably secure a depression diagnosis from a clinical psychologist. For the record, I LOVE Eeyore. However, here is the trouble. Over my years as a special education teacher, I have encountered many team members who suffer from 'Eeyore' syndrome. Nothing is ever right. Every step forward elicits a comment about two steps back. These individuals tend to be cynical and struggle with hope. Often, the target of their discontent is things outside of their control which are implicit in the education process.

As a special education teacher and a mom, I try not to fall into an 'Eeyore' mindset. It's easier to do than you think. There will be little things that bug you. There will be big things that drive you batty. Don't let them get to you. Constant complaining brings everyone down and keeps you stuck in negativity. Every day you wake up, you have the choice of whether you want to help bring a positive mindset to the overall life experience of your child, or bring them down with negativity. Now, does this mean that you have to be in a great mood every day? Of course not. You're human, and you will have down moments at times. It does mean that you can do your best to flip the script when you are grumpy instead of spreading that 'Eeyore' energy. If you are struggling, reference the tools and strategies listed in part 3 of this book to connect with your own beautiful heart and find your happiness. I truly believe positive energy is contagious.

Accept or Advocate?

Read each situation and describe the action you would take. Would you accept the situation or advocate for change? Explain your thinking to reflect on your personal advocacy skills.

Situation: Your child's case manager expresses that they have a very large caseload and may be stretched for time during the school year. They express that they will try their best to meet everyone's needs.	
What would you accept about the situation?	Where might you advocate for change and how might this take place?

Situation: Your child is struggling with a particular concept in math and is having trouble getting the help they need. Your child reports that he has asked for the teacher's help multiple times.	
What would you accept about the situation?	Where might you advocate for change and how might this take place?

Situation: Your child expresses that they are having a hard time finding a friend to sit with at lunch so they are simply listening to their music instead. They say it's a little bit lonely, but it's not a big deal. You are concerned that they are experiencing embarrassment or exclusion.	
What would you accept about the situation?	Where might you advocate for change and how might this take place?

Situation: An administrator shares information about another student during an IEP meeting which violates data privacy. You aren't sure whether you should let him know that this is a problem.	
What would you accept about the situation?	Where might you advocate for change and how might this take place?

Situation: Another parent warns you that a particular teacher isn't very effective in working with students with special needs. Your child has been assigned to this teacher.	
What would you accept about the situation?	Where might you advocate for change and how might this take place?

Situation: Your child's school has implemented a new grading policy and it doesn't really make sense to you. You have some concerns about how it might impact your child's learning process.	
What would you accept about the situation?	Where might you advocate for change and how might this take place?

Does this mean we shy away from advocacy and accept our roles as they are? Certainly not. It does mean that we fix our eyes on the good as much as possible. When the good could be better through wise advocacy, we take steps to make things happen and affect positive change. The important thing to remember is that we must be selective regarding the situations and needs we choose to advocate for. If we constantly advocate in situations which we could have solved for ourselves, or which just aren't priority problems, we may overwhelm the team and create difficulty with getting our voices heard when there is a true need.

> If we constantly advocate in situations which we could have solved for ourselves, or which just aren't priority problems, we may overwhelm the team and create difficulty with getting our voices heard when there is a true need.

Activity 18 provides an activity you may complete to determine what you would accept and where you would advocate in various situations. Use this to bolster your skills in wise advocacy decisions. Also, see Chapter 10 to learn more about the power of acceptance to generate contentment and joy in your life.

Conclusion

My grandmother always told me, 'You catch more flies with honey than vinegar.' In many situations, you will need to speak up for your child or encourage them to speak up for themself. Finding a way to engage in advocacy which is kind, diplomatic, and assertive can result in better outcomes for all team members. Most importantly, it can mean that healthy collaboration takes place for the betterment of your child's education. Start with a commitment to assume positive intent from the members of your child's team. Engage your active listening skills to ensure full understanding of messages. Stay mindful and calm as much as you can, because sometimes our emotions can result in impulsive communication we later regret.

As you work with the school, share what you can offer about your child in order to solve problems before they start. Cultivate your ability to be assertive without being too aggressive or too passive in conversations. Your voice matters most, along with the voice of your child, in making sure the IEP works best for the little human being who has to live it each day. You can help your child find their voice by teaching them to use 'I statements' and by cultivating self-determination skills. Try not to do or say things for your child which they could do or say for themselves. Invite them to have a vision for their future and put them in the driver's seat as much as possible. Finally, try to adhere to a positive mindset in which you are selective about where and when you advocate. Not all problems can be solved, sadly, and at times it is best to choose acceptance instead. Not easy, but very helpful for your own personal peace.

Chapter 3 Simple Snapshot

◆ 'Assuming positive intent' means that we believe all team members are doing the best they can with the tools and resources they have.

- ◆ Active listening means that instead of interrupting or formulating your reply, you are fully taking in the message of the person speaking.
- ◆ Being proactive requires a reflection on past patterns to inform potential future problems. Solve problems before they start by sharing about your child's patterns to help the team.
- ◆ Assertiveness is important and involves sharing information in a way that is clear and that does not make others feel judged, blamed, or attacked.
- ◆ Invite your child to create a vision for the person they want to be. Then, help them find their voice to ask for the resources and tools they need to get there.
- ◆ Evaluate situations which don't 'sit well' with you and decide carefully whether to accept or advocate. Try to see the good in situations as much as you possibly can.

Chapter 3 Reflection Questions

Use the following questions to reflect on what you have learned in the chapter. You may choose to journal about them or discuss them with a partner or small group to gain further insights.

1. What are some of your child's patterns over the course of the school year seasons? How might this information help their IEP team?
2. What are your thoughts on the premise 'assume positive intent'? Where might this be helpful and what problems might you foresee with this philosophy?
3. Do you tend toward a passive, assertive, or aggressive communication style? How might you continue to cultivate assertiveness to get your voice heard?
4. Where do you 'catch' yourself doing things or saying things your child could do or say for themselves? How might you remind yourself to foster independence in these areas?

5. What are some dreams you have for your child and what are some dreams they hold for themself? What resources or tools might they need to achieve these hopes?
6. What might be some areas in which advocacy is needed at this time in your life or the life of your child? What are some situations you need to accept at this time?

References

Cayoun, B., Shires, A., & Francis, S. (2018). Mindful communication skills. *The Clinical Handbook of Mindfulness-integrated Cognitive Behavior Therapy*, pp. 255–276, doi:10.1002/9781119389675.ch11.

Crandall, D. & Kincaid, M. (2017). *Permission to speak freely: How the best leaders cultivate a culture of candor*. Oakland, CA: Berrett-Koehler Publishers.

Da Fonte, M.A. & Barton-Arwood, S.M. (2017). Collaboration of general and special education teachers: Perspectives and strategies. *Intervention in School and Clinic*, vol. 53, no. 2, pp. 99–106, doi:10.1177/1053451217693370.

Desai, M. (2018). Module 5 sensitive interpersonal communication skills. *Introduction to Rights-Based Direct Practice with Children*, pp. 129–150, doi:10.1007/978-981-10-4729-9_5.

DuFour, R., DuFour, R., Eaker, R., Many, T.W., & Mattos, M. (2016). *Learning by doing*. Bloomington, IN: Solution Tree Press.

Kabat-Zinn, J. (2016). *Mindfulness for beginners: Reclaiming the present moment and your life*. Boulder, CO: Sounds True.

Lopez, N., Uphold, N., Douglas, K., & Freeman-Green, S. (2020). Teaching high school students with disabilities to advocate for academic accommodations. *The Journal of Special Education*, vol. 54, no. 3, pp. 146–156, doi:10.1177/0022466919892955.

Merriam-Webster. (2021). Advocacy. In *Merriam-Webster.com*. Retrieved October 28, 2021, from https://www.merriam-webster.com/dictionary/advocacy.

Milne, A.A. 1. (1954). *Winnie-the-pooh*. Dutton.

McAdamis, S. (2013). *Listening: The forgotten skill necessary for effective collaboration*. All Things PLC. https://www.allthingsplc.info/blog/view/19/listening-the-forgotten-skill-necessary-for-effective-collaboration.

National Parent Center on Transition and Employment. (2019). *Self-determination*. Pacer.org. https://www.pacer.org/transition/learning-center/independent-community-living/self-determination.asp.

Supiano, B. (2021). *The problem with venting about your students*. The Chronicle of Higher Education. Retrieved September 3, 2022, from https://www.chronicle.com/article/the-problem-with-venting-about-your-students.

Suttie, J. (2021). Does venting your feelings actually help? *Greater Good Magazine*. https://greatergood.berkeley.edu/article/item/does_venting_your_feelings_actually_help.

Vogelsinger, B. (2016). *Five engaging uses for letters in your classroom*. Edutopia.org. https://www.edutopia.org/blog/uses-for-letters-in-classroom-brett-vogelsinger.

Yirmiya, N. & Seidman, I. (2021) Empathy. *Encyclopedia of Autism Spectrum Disorders*, Springer International Publishing, 2021, pp. 1730–1737, doi:10.1007/978-3-319-91280-6_1729.

II

Connecting with Your Child

Welcome to our second section: Connecting with Your Child. As our children grow and develop, our role in their lives must change right along with them. This section will offer strategies and approaches which may support you in maintaining a positive, hope-giving relationship with your child even as you navigate the difficulties of life together. Together you can explore the basic needs which drive each member of your family to bolster your connections. You can identify and celebrate the strengths of your family and develop a regular plan for celebration and shared enjoyment. This section also acknowledges that at times, your child may struggle with undesirable behavior and this can create challenges for you as a parent. Here you will find intervention strategies to help mitigate undesirable behavior and create a more peaceful home. This sets the stage for school success as children grow in their self-management skills. The section closes with a series of activities which can help to unify your family and to come together to identify the characteristics which make your family wonderful. The ultimate goal of this section is for you to help your child know who they are and how deeply they are loved and supported. All of this will offer a foundation for lasting success for your unique, incredible child!

DOI: 10.4324/9781003364443-6

4

Cultivating Connection

Rebekah James was an extrovert. She was a social creature from the day she was born, and she was constantly surrounded by friends. Being around people gave her energy and satisfaction, and she found that if she spent too much time alone, she started to feel down and drained. From an early age, Rebekah knew that she was a people person and she needed to work in a highly interactive profession. She found a job which matched her style and continued to fill her social calendar with as much interaction as possible.

When Rebekah had her first child, Sasha, she loaded their days with social events. She joined 'Mommy and Me' groups and planned lots of play dates for Sasha. Signing Sasha up for lots of activities gave her the chance to connect with other moms and have fun conversations while their children enjoyed their time together. Rebekah continued this busy social scheduling for years, constantly filling up Sasha's time with interaction. That is, until everything came to a screeching halt.

Sasha was in 7th grade. She was starting to become her own person and she was developing interests like sports. She especially liked soccer and enjoyed being a part of her team. Rebekah continued to work and thrive as a social butterfly. One day, Sasha and Rebekah hopped in the car for a coffee date with a friend and her daughter. On the way there, Sasha seemed somewhat sad.

"What's going on?" Rebekah asked, "Are you okay?"

"Well, mom, sometimes I wish I could just stay home," Sasha replied.

"What do you mean? It will be fun. You can't just sit on the couch all day," Rebekah replied without much thought, pulling into the parking lot of the coffee shop. They entered and Rebekah warmly greeted her friend. Sasha slumped in and sat down silently in a chair in the corner.

"Sasha, what's your order?" Rebekah asked.

"I don't want anything," Sasha replied with an edge of irritation in her voice.

"Okay…" Rebekah was concerned. This was so unlike Sasha and usually she loved her hot chocolate. As the coffee date unfolded, Rebekah was her usual animated self, chatting with her mom friend about all of the updates of life. Sasha sat quietly in the corner, choosing not to interact with anyone. Thankfully, both girls had phones along so they quietly scrolled as their moms chatted away. The

DOI: 10.4324/9781003364443-7

time passed, the adults wrapped up their conversation, and they parted ways. On the car ride home, Rebekah couldn't hide her irritation.

"Sasha, that was pretty rude. You didn't even talk to anyone," Rebekah chided her.

"Mom, I told you I didn't want to go. I'm just not as social as you are. I don't always want to be around people," Sasha expressed.

This gave Rebekah pause. Sasha had never stated this before so clearly. It made complete sense. Sasha enjoyed interacting with her soccer team and got along well with other students at school, but she definitely wasn't as social and seemed to gain energy from spending time alone. Being more introverted was a foreign concept to Rebekah, but this seemed to be Sasha's style. From then on, Rebekah didn't drag Sasha along on her coffee dates or try to force social interaction into Sasha's life. She let go and decided to let Sasha be her wonderful, quiet, creative, unique self. This had lasting positive results in their connection and relationship.

Rebekah had the best of intentions in scheduling lots of social events for her daughter. Why? Because social interaction met Rebekah's needs and helped her to enjoy life. However, this was not the case for Sasha. As we set the stage for our children to grow and thrive, it can help us tremendously to explore who our children truly are and the needs which drive their actions. The better we get to know their needs, preferences, and interests, the better we can support their development and communicate what they need to school personnel. This chapter will provide you with strategies to get to know your child better and cultivate a connection with who they are. Sometimes we fail to fully 'see' our child because we are too caught up in our own views

Key Themes

◆ All human beings are born with innate survival needs such as food, water, shelter, and clothing, and when these go unmet, learning and development may pause.

◆ Once these basic needs are met, human beings tend toward additional needs which drive their development such as fun, freedom, autonomy, and belonging.

◆ Uncovering what a child likes and prefers can help unlock key information to meet their needs both at home and at school.

◆ In order to qualify for special education, learning challenges must be evident, and thus, students may internalize a negative perception of themselves or their capabilities.

◆ Parents can work with their children to help them write a new story which includes hope in their capacity for learning and success.

on what human beings need and how they thrive. Open your heart and your mind as you experience the activities included here, and you might just discover fun new information about your child which can help you enjoy parenting!

Planting Seeds, Sustaining Hope

Every single day, you are planting seeds with your child. Every time you cultivate a new ability, model a social or emotional skill, or even offer a connective investment through empathy, a seed may be planted. Sometimes, it seems as if these seeds are falling among the rocks, and they will never grow. Sometimes, it seems like a drought has descended and they will dry up and die. The most happy and content parents I know believe that most of the time, those seeds flourish into something helpful and meaningful for their child. The truth is, it may be many years before you get to see the seeds you have sown develop into fully sprouted plants, but rest assured, they are out there somewhere growing and thriving and basking in the sunshine.

With this understanding, you can sustain yourself best when you tend to your sense of hope in your child's future and in your own potential impact. Hope is one of the most critical elements of sustained happiness in parenting a child with special education needs. As a parent, you engage in small acts of hope every single day, often without realizing it. Teaching a new skill is an act of hope that your child will learn and grow. Showing up for an Individual Education Planning meeting is an act of hope that the team will find ways to make school a better experience for the student. Even getting out of bed each morning is an act of hope when times are tough and you just want to give up and shut out the world. We've all been there.

> You can choose each day to grow more cynical or more hopeful. You can let the difficulties drag you down, or you can look forward to the possibilities which exist for your child.

You can choose each day to grow more cynical or more hopeful. You can let the difficulties drag you down, or you can look forward to the possibilities which exist for your child. It helps to remember that parents don't always get to see the successes immediately, and that's just part of the deal. Somewhere deep within your child's heart, a seed you lovingly planted might just be preparing to leverage them into the mightiest oak in the forest. Rest assured that by showing up for your child and never giving up, you are doing enough. I promise.

Needs Drive the Bus

Human beings are not empty boxes waiting to be motivated by external forces. Rather, individuals take action based on a series of innate needs. The most important element which indicates the individual's feeling of happiness or sorrow is the extent to which basic needs are met. If even one area of need is unmet, the individual may feel ill at ease which may impede learning and development. Yikes. What does this mean for you as a parent? It means that part of your task is to explore the unmet needs which exist within your child and take steps to meet them as much as you can. As your child grows older, the hope is that they learn strategies and skills to meet their own needs as much as possible.

One of the most universal needs I have discovered over the years among my students in special education is the need for FUN. People, especially those of the younger variety, are hard-wired to desire laughter and pleasure. According to Dr. William Glasser, human beings are genetically wired to meet certain needs including fun or enjoyment, and this is universal across cultures (Wubbolding, 2015). Unfortunately, by the time students reach placement in special education, most students have probably had some intensely difficult experiences at school. To qualify for services, schools must officially prove that things aren't working for the student as they are. Somewhere along the line, students have realized that things just aren't working for them the way they seem to work for other students. This is painful and even traumatic for so many students. Compounding this with the fact that peers tend to perceive when someone is different and can be quite cruel, you have a recipe for a true disaster in the lives of students in need of special education services. Once they qualify, students may experience even further difficulty as they wrestle with the stigma surrounding the concept of disability and the ableism which is alive and well in our schools and society. This all sounds quite bleak indeed.

As a parent, there is nothing more painful than watching your child endure struggles which you can't 'fix' or resolve for them. Yet, there is hope. You can help your child as they experience their initial placement in special education programming by focusing on FUN in the home setting. Your home can become a space of healing, recovery, and FUN for your child! As a parent, you have the unique opportunity to completely shift the narrative from one of pain and struggle to one of hope and success. Creating fun and relaxing experiences at home can make a world of difference for your child and can also support your own health and happiness as a parent.

> Here is the GREAT news: Your home can become a space of healing, recovery, and FUN for your child!

How might you begin to create a fun environment in your home? It starts with empathy. Pause to take an honest look at what you are doing and put yourself in your child's shoes. Lengthy chore lists? Not fun. Overscheduling activities? Not fun. Strict and detailed rules? Not fun. As children struggle at school, it may be time to loosen the reins a bit at home and relax on expectations like chores or stringent rules. Your child needs a space to decompress and just 'be,' so pushing them to do things they don't want to do may backfire. Infuse your parenting with warmth and love so that you can help your child unwind. It's okay to ditch your usual parenting practices and mix things up. Fearlessly try new things, and you will be surprised by the positive outcomes for your child.

I recommend that you think back to yourself as a child when thinking about bringing fun to your home, imagining yourself when they were young. Perhaps you were high energy, chatty, partial to a good time, rambunctious, and perhaps not the greatest listener? Yes, I am definitely describing myself circa third grade. Thinking about my earliest memories of home, I remember many 'time-outs' in my room when I got to be too much. I remember perceiving that I just couldn't do anything right. I remember frequent trips to the park just to get away and take a breath. I remember a frustrated mother who didn't know what to do with my energy and my busy brain. As a mother today, these memories help me to implement the exact opposite practices with my own children. Above all else, I want them to know that they are capable, valued, and loved. This sometimes means relaxing on chores, rules, and control.

We must learn to accept our child's basic need for fun and bring this into their home experiences as much as possible. They just weren't built to be robots, and this isn't what we want for them anyway. So, what's the answer? To create interactive,

TABLE 4.1 Practical Ideas for Bringing Fun into Learning Experiences for Students

Ideas to Use Humor	Ideas to Use Novelty
Use a Joke of the Day and invite your child to share cheesy jokes as well. Fun riddles also work well.	Once you have established a routine, switch things up at times to incorporate preferred activities on occasion.
Tell your child about the things that make you smile and invite them to share the same. Laugh at yourself often!	Surprise your child with a random funny hat or costume. Sometimes, the best gift you can offer them is your own goofiness as a parent.
Share in laughter at funny pieces of media such as YouTube clips or Tik Toks to bring laughter and lightness into your home, especially if there have been struggles.	If something isn't working, change it! Think outside the box with your approach and try new things. Getting 'stuck in a rut' helps no one.
Ideas to Offer Preferred Activities Talk often about what interests your child and try to find activities for them to engage in outside of school.	Ideas for 'Game-like' Experiences Find games you enjoy to play with your child which are NOT on a screen. Good old-fashioned board games actually involve great learning opportunities.
Work in time for your child's preferred activities even when you are busy and encourage them to find hobbies they enjoy.	Intersperse odd trivia questions in the day to catch your child's interest.
Incorporate your child's interests in your home as much as possible. Get creative and invite them to share ideas on how to do this.	Watch game shows together and try to guess the answers before the contestants! Fun and cognitively engaging.

meaningful, interesting experiences in which children have the chance to relax and feel a sense of connection and deep belonging in our families. Infusing your home with humor, engaging your child in preferred activities, mixing things up with novelty, and 'game-ifying' the environment can help your home become a more enjoyable space for everyone. Table 4.1 offers practical ideas to bring fun into home experiences for children at any age level and with any types of special needs.

While the need for fun is common and can be very helpful for your family, it is also helpful to explore other areas of need which may be driving your child. Love, power, and freedom are other natural human desires which may greatly influence development. It can be very helpful to determine which areas are most important to the members of your family so you can better understand each other. Activity 19 offers a 'Basic Needs Assessment' you can use to reflect on your primary needs together.

Another way to send the message that you care about your child and you want to meet their needs may involve tools to bring out their individual perspectives. As parents, it's easy to assume that we know all there is to know about our children, but this is not always the case. Activities 20 and 21 offer opportunities for you to learn more about your child and discover windows into their personal internal worlds. You can complete each activity as well in order to share about yourself. You may use the information you gather to exercise greater empathy for your child, incorporate their preferences, and share more deeply about who you are. The hope is that you will uncover helpful new knowledge about your child while you convey the message: 'I care about who you are.' This can also be a powerful experience to deepen your connection and mutual understanding, which is a beautiful thing!

The information you uncover using these tools may also help your child's school. Gathering information and sharing it with your child's teachers may help them understand what needs drive their actions. Bringing the school world and the out-of-school life together may help your child excel, as they experience greater consistency and school faculty have key information on their needs. Remember that you and school personnel are partners with the same goal: the child's lasting success. This

Basic Needs Assessment

Complete this activity as a family to get to know the key needs for each person!

There are 5 basic needs that everybody has:

- Survival/Security
- Freedom
- Fun
- Love/Belonging
- Power

To have a balanced life we strive to meet all of these needs. Examples of each area include:

Survival	Freedom	Fun	Love	Power
Food	Choice	Play	Belonging	Achievement
Clothing	Creativity	Humor	Caring	Self Control
Rest	Change	Joy	Sharing	Importance
Shelter	Flexibility	Excitement	Cooperating	Significance
Safety	Adaptability	Enthusiasm	Sharing	Capability
Health	Travel	Novelty	Joining	Competition

Note that the need for survival is important for everyone. Once these basic needs are met, the other four areas become the driving forces behind human behavior. Most people have a preferred area which motivates their actions.

Have each member of your family complete the 'Basic Needs Assessment' on the following pages. Each participant should tally their score in order to identify which need areas are strongest in their lives.

Then, reflect together using the questions provided.

1= Not True 3= Sometimes 5=True	1	3	5
1. I love to make friends.			
2. It's easy for me to talk to anyone.			
3. I like to talk on the phone.			
4. I like to work with other people.			
5. I spend a lot of time with people.			
6. I want people to like me.			
7. I want people to be proud of me.			
8. What my friends think about me is important.			

9. I prefer working with a group to working alone.			
10. I like meeting new people.			
11. I don't like making mistakes			
12. I like to watch others before I try something new.			
13. I don't like change.			
14. I want my desk or room kept neat.			
15. I want to be very good at what I do.			
16. How I look is important to me.			
17. I worry about trying new things.			
18. I like to be 'right.'			
19. I like to organize and lead activities.			
20. It bothers me if things aren't the way I want.			
21. I like to have choices.			
22. I am an active person.			
23. Sitting at school is hard for me.			
24. I don't like to read for a long time.			
25. I love to try new things.			
26. I will hang out alone if I feel like it.			
27. What I wear doesn't matter to me.			
28. I am comfortable doing things alone.			
29. I don't like being told what to do.			
30. Being neat and tidy doesn't matter to me.			
31. I laugh a lot.			
32. I have collections.			
33. I like to tell jokes.			
34. I like to make people laugh.			
35. People think I'm goofy.			
36. I like to play games.			
37. I find a lot of things funny.			
38. I think school is fun.			

ACTIVITY NINETEEN CONTINUED

39. I like to sing/dance along with music.			
40. People think I am funny			

Scoring:

Total #'s 1 -10	Total #'s 11 -20	Total #'s 21 -30	Total #'s 31 -40
LOVE	POWER	FREEDOM	FUN

Which area was most strong for you? Which was the lowest? The following summarizes what your results may mean.

Love: It is important that you feel liked. You are sociable and you work hard for others. You enjoy working in a group. You can meet your needs through interaction.

Power: You like to feel in control. You observe situations before jumping in and you feel bothered if you make a mistake. You like to be organized and on top of things.

Freedom: You like to have choices and you need opportunities to be up and moving. You love to experiment and try new things.

Fun: You always want to enjoy yourself, no matter where you are or what you are doing. You like to play games and you are an entertainer.

Questions for Personal Reflection	
What are your thoughts on your results? Are you surprised? Was this expected? Explain.	
What are some ways you can meet your strongest need areas in your life?	

Family Needs Summary			
List the names of family members under their strongest need area:			
LOVE	POWER	FREEDOM	FUN
What are the strongest needs in our family and how can we meet those needs together?			
What are some ways we can help meet these needs in other environments such as school?			

perspective is energizing and inspiring! I hope you enjoy using the following tools to learn more about your child and that you find avenues to share this new knowledge with your child's support team at school.

Empower Your Child

In certain circles, the concept of success is a synonym for wealth. In the world of sports, it's the best statistics. In the theater, it's a sold-out show with a standing ovation to top it off. For pop stars, it's record sales. For chefs, it's a good review. For computer technicians, it's a functioning system. The idea of 'success' is relative and highly contextual. There is no one metric to define it, and

Use this form to share about your current favorites. Each family member may complete and share. Save as a snapshot to revisit later in life!

My Favorites

Name: _____   Date: _____

Tell me all about your favorites, your dreams and your best moments!

1. **Favorite Things** _____
   _____
   _____

2. **Favorite People** _____
   _____
   _____

3. **Favorite Pets** _____
   _____
   _____

4. **Dream Job** _____
   _____
   _____

5. **Favorite Places** _____
   _____
   _____

6. **Favorite School Subject** _____
   _____
   _____

7. **I Like it When Adults Are:** _____
   _____
   _____

8. **In the future, I hope I can buy my own:** _____
   _____
   _____

What Matters to Me

Name: _____ Date: _____

Answer the following questions to share about what matters most in your life.

1. **What do you value most in your life?**

   _____

   _____

   _____

   _____

2. **Who are the most important people in your life?**

   _____

   _____

   _____

   _____

3. **What traits would you have if you could be anyone you wanted?**

   _____

   _____

   _____

4. **What is your dream job?**

   _____

   _____

   _____

5. **What are some accomplishments you are proud of?**

   _____

   _____

   _____

6. What is the highlight of your life so far, or your best moment?

_____

_____

_____

7. What qualities do you look for in a friend?

_____

_____

_____

8. What gives your life meaning?

_____

_____

_____

9. If you didn't need to make money, what would you do with your time?

_____

_____

_____

10. Describe your dream parent-what do they do? How do they act?

_____

_____

_____

11. What do you love about our family? Why do you love it?

_____

_____

_____

12. What can I do as a parent to help you succeed?

_____

_____

_____

everyone has their own version in their minds. In your journey with your child, the idea of 'success' is going to look completely different based on their individualized needs. Many have tried and failed to create sweeping definitions of success for children (such as scores on standardized tests), but no single tool can measure the myriad of ways a child can succeed. For one child, it may be tying her shoes on her own. For another, it may be engaging in an impromptu social conversation. As a parent, you will help yourself and your child when you develop a realistic definition of success aligned to your child's needs. The key is to figure out that 'sweet spot' where your child is challenged to grow, but not overwhelmed to the point of frustration. In this balanced space, children can make incredible gains. Expecting baby steps in terms of progress is a much healthier and life-giving approach, rather than expecting leaps and bounds.

> In your journey with your child, the idea of 'success' is going to look completely different based on their individualized needs.

Academic success is important, certainly, but too often our children receive the message that if they don't naturally and easily understand the content at school, there is something wrong with them. Children respond by trying to avoid academics to protect themselves from further pain, frustration, and embarrassment. Far too many children have developed defense mechanisms to manage the difficulties they experience at school. A defense mechanism is a strategy used to ward off threats and reduce anxiety, and people often employ them without even realizing it (Ewen, 2014). Essentially, children lose who they are in the face of stress. They've lost their joy and they spend their school day in an uncomfortable state of 'red alert' looking for the next problem. At home, it becomes even more important to offer a space of peace and healing. It may also be helpful to support school staff in identifying the defense mechanisms our child may be using to avoid embarrassment, shame, or struggle. Table 4.2 offers suggestions for ways you can convey your investment and hope for the child when you realize they are utilizing a defense mechanism.

TABLE 4.2 Conveying Parental Investment When Children Utilize Defense Mechanisms

Common Defense Mechanisms Among Children	How Parents Can Convey Messages of Support and Hope
Refusing to attempt an academic task to hide the fact that they do not have the skills to complete it.	With a lighthearted approach, encourage children to give the task a try, offering to stand by in order to help if necessary.
'Testing' limits with new adults to determine whether or not they are trustworthy. This may involve questioning teachers, defying teachers, or even insulting teachers at times.	Encourage your child to view teachers as trustworthy resources who are there to help them. No matter how you feel about a particular teacher, only share positive messages about educators with your child.
Withdrawing from others or disconnecting when they feel overstimulated, overwhelmed, or stressed during class.	Give space and allow your child to withdraw for a bit. Then, express that you miss them and you love spending time with them, again, with a warm tone.
Rocking in chairs, climbing on furniture, tearing up paper, chewing pencils, or other physical activities which may create undesirable messes in your home. This may be related to sensory needs or a desire for movement.	Discover approaches to meet your child's sensory needs such as weighted blankets, physical exercise, fidget items, and chewing gum. If you see your child engaging in these actions, dim the lights and lower the volume of auditory input in your home.
Pretending to be capable of academic skills in order to avoid working on them and facing difficulty. Children may deflect targeting certain skills and accept low scores in these areas.	Continuously express how much you care about your child's learning and believe in their potential for success. Encourage them to give their best effort and expect mistakes in the learning process. Uphold the mantra, "We Love Our Mistakes."

All of these efforts are designed to help your child grow in self-acceptance. Through empowering conversation and modeling, you can show them that they can find belonging and self-worth without using their old defense mechanisms. Children realize that they get back what they give out, and that life is easier when they learn to get along with the people who surround them and trust the goodness available in the world. As a parent, there may be nothing more rewarding than identifying and mitigating a defense mechanism to see your child grow and thrive.

As you uncover defense mechanisms, share them with your child's teachers. This can be extremely helpful to unlock school success. Encourage teachers to build trust with your child if there is a history of trauma or attachment difficulties. Help teachers understand gaps in skills if you are aware of them so that they can help to fill in the gaps. When you come together with teachers in this manner, you show your child that you are 100% on their side in the journey to make school a positive place. Children need to understand that they have someone in their corner to help them fight through the obstacles that have created difficulty in the past. As you participate in the special education process, the hope is that it can give them a fresh start and help them see themselves and their school experience with new eyes. Special education can become a space to empower them and celebrate who they are! We can help them realize that they are fully accepted, that everyone has issues to deal with, and that they don't have to keep their guard up at school any longer.

As a parent, your messaging about school and special education is powerful. I can't emphasize this point enough. I have a dear friend whose children enjoy the dentist. Why? Because from their very first dentist visit, he persuaded them that going to the dentist was a blast and that they would love having nice clean teeth. In turn, if you highlight the positive aspects of school and see special education as a positive opportunity, your child may follow suit and experience better outcomes. There may be nothing more rewarding than seeing a young person transform from lost and struggling to peaceful and engaged in the school environment, and special education services can achieve just that. A person at peace can live in harmony with other people, grow in integrity, and develop a positive identity. Once we help our children establish the person they want to be, everything else falls into place. Academics improve because children become more willing to take risks and invest themselves in new challenges. Relationships improve because children don't have to use their old defense mechanisms to push people away. I have seen this happen many times, and it's an absolutely beautiful thing!

Help Your Child Write a New Story

As human beings, each of us is trying to make sense out of the world around us. We create stories to help us understand the world and we live as the main characters in our own narratives. Our children have their own internal stories which guide their perceptions of the world in which they are the protagonist. The stories they are telling themselves may actually dictate their potential for success. So much in life is determined by what individuals believe about themselves. According to Robert K. Merton, a self-fulfilling prophecy is "a false definition of the situation evoking a new behavior which makes the originally false conception come true" (Lopez, 2017). To put it simply, what we believe about ourselves is often what we become. This phenomenon rings true for children today. What they believe about themselves often determines what they become. Too often, they hold false beliefs about their capabilities and sell themselves short. This in turn prevents them from fulfilling their full potential. They are telling themselves stories which hold them back from success.

> To put it simply, what we believe about ourselves is often what we become.

As a parent, it is tremendously helpful to uncover and identify the limiting stories your child may be telling themself. There are many examples of limiting stories you may find within your child's mind and heart. 'I'm no good at school.' Limiting story. 'I have a disability so I won't ever be able to succeed.' Limiting story. 'I'm just not good enough.' Limiting story. 'I'm afraid of the future because I probably won't succeed.' Limiting story. These limiting stories are most often serving as self-fulfilling prophecies in their lives which keep them stuck. Initially, the discovery of such stories may feel overwhelming and painful. Over my years as a special education teacher, I have come to view these limiting stories as opportunities rather than problems. Once discovered, this is your chance to help your child see that the stories which limit them do not hold truth and do not have to dictate their words, thoughts, and actions. You can encourage them, lift them up, and let them know that it is time to WRITE A NEW STORY!

In my practice, the process usually follows a similar pattern. First, I spend time building rapport and trust with the student so that they are willing to openly share with me. Second, we explore their current perspective on school and their past struggles in order to uncover any stories which may be limiting them. Third, we talk about a new more optimistic story which focuses on overcoming past challenges, capitalizing on strengths, and hope-giving beliefs. Finally, we work together to make the new and better story come true. Over and over and over again, I have seen this process TRANSFORM my students. It's absolutely amazing. In fact, this may be the single most powerful element of my practice which keeps me teaching special education year after year. You can engage in a similar process as a parent. Trust me, it is worth the investment. Helping your child write a new story is a beautiful act of HOPE both on the part of the parent and on the part of the child.

> Helping your child write a new story is a beautiful act of HOPE both on the part of the parent and on the part of the child.

One of the most important things we can do for children is to give them hope. But here's the thing, we can't give away what we don't have. I encourage you to decide early and often that you are going to stay hopeful even when your child is facing the greatest difficulties. As you begin to explore the limiting beliefs your child holds, you may be surprised at how hopeless and dire the situation may seem. Even in these difficulties, I have learned that with love, care, and thoughtful intervention, we can bring out the best in every individual. Some days, keeping hope alive is the toughest part of our role as parents. On such days, we can say to ourselves, "My best is enough." Your best effort and love are sufficient, so stay strong.

Often, when people hear that someone is parenting a child with special education needs, they tend to say something like: "Oh, you must have the patience of a saint." This sweeping generalization is often far from accurate, but the sentiment is somewhat correct.

Write a New Story

*Name:*_____

Complete the following sentences:

Past Negative Thinking:

1. In the past, I have struggled with _____

_____

_____

_____

_____

2. I have worried about _____

_____

_____

3. I have a hard time believing in myself when it comes to _____

_____

_____

_____

_____

My New Story:

1. I believe that I will overcome my struggles by _____

_____

_____

_____

_____

2. I have many strengths and I am capable of _____

_____

_____

3. I believe that I will _____

_____

_____

_____

_____

When it comes to parenting a child with special needs, patience takes on a different form. We connect with the school to create a plan, put it in place, and then wait to see if it works. As parents, we try to support learning as much as we can at home, holding out hope that we can contribute to our child's success. Again, focus on baby steps and don't anticipate overnight transformation. Patience and realistic expectations will keep you strong.

With hearts full of hope and a commitment to care for our children, we can unlock the new stories which will cause them to find success. The self-fulfilling prophecy can work both ways. Just as a negative belief may come true, a positive and hopeful story can come to fruition when we persuade our children to believe in it with their full hearts. Activity 22: My New Story helps you walk through this hope-giving process with your child. The future dividends may be success beyond previous limited expectations.

Conclusion

The most powerful factor which will sustain you in your life as a parent is the belief that you are making a lasting positive impact on your child. Dig into the needs which drive each member of your family and strive to come together to create a life which aligns to everyone's basic needs. Remember that what makes your child 'tick' may be very different from the things you value. Children need to feel seen and supported, even when they are very different from their parents in personality and preferences. We are all different, and that is part of what makes life so beautiful! Fully accept and celebrate who your child is, and watch them thrive.

One of the most common needs we all share is a need for enjoyment and fun. Reflect on ideas to infuse fun in your home whenever you can, and you will feel a lighter load in general. Explore what matters most to your child and continuously get to know their favorite things. They will grow and their interests will change, and it's up to you as a parent to stay up-to-date as much as you can. See your child as individuals who have the potential for greatness and help them write a new story for their lives. Too many children limit themselves with negative stories about their potential. You have the chance to give them a completely new outlook, helping them embrace school as a place where they can succeed with the right support. Give yourself a daily pep talk in which you choose hope over cynicism. Hope in the seeds you are planting with your child. Believe in the growth that is happening whether you get to see it immediately or not. Trust me, showing up for your child with love is often MORE than enough!

Chapter 4 Simple Snapshot

- ◆ Most human behavior is need-based. Exploring the needs which motivate each member of your family may help you connect more deeply.
- ◆ Invest in understanding the needs, preferences, and interests of your child as much as possible.
- ◆ The things which matter most to you may not matter as much to your child. Find a common ground in which to come together.
- ◆ We all tell ourselves stories in our minds to make sense of the world around us.
- ◆ Your child may be believing a negative story about their own capabilities.

♦ Support your child in 'writing a new story' for their lives based on hope and the unshakeable belief that life can be enjoyable and positive.

Chapter 4 Reflection Questions

Use the following questions to reflect on what you have learned in the chapter. You may choose to journal about them or discuss them with a partner or small group to gain further insights.

1. What do you love most about being a parent? What motivates you to keep going when things get difficult?
2. What are some ways you are similar to your child? What are some ways you are different?
3. Which of the basic needs are most prominent for you? How might this impact your parenting?
4. Which of the basic needs are most prominent for your child? How does this show up in their actions, words, thoughts, and perspectives?
5. What are your perspectives on what matters to you? How are these similar and different to the values and priorities of your child?
6. What are some negative or limiting beliefs your child has held in the past? How might you help them write a new success story focused on the positive?

References

Ewen, R.B. (2014). *An introduction to theories of personality*. 7th ed. Hove, East Sussex: Psychology Press.

Lopez, F. (2017). Altering the trajectory of the self-fulfilling prophecy: Asset-based pedagogy and classroom dynamics. *Journal of Teacher Education*, vol. 68, no. 2, pp. 193–212, doi:10.1177/0022487116685751.

Wubbolding, R.E. (2015). The voice of William Glasser: Accessing the continuing evolution of reality therapy. *Journal of Mental Health Counseling*, vol. 37, no. 3, pp. 189–205, doi:10.17744/mehc.37.3.01.

5

Redefine Success

As a high school special education teacher, one of the toughest parts of Kim Xiong's job was when it was time to send her seniors on to the next phase of life. Over her four years with her students, she developed such a close relationship with each of them and their families, it was tough to see them go. In late winter, she scheduled a meeting with each family to talk about their student's transition to adult life. For most of them, they would move on to a program for 18–21 year old students who need more time to work on their goals before leaving the school setting. This program was awesome and she always felt great about sending her students there! They would work on life skills, functional academics and job training on a daily basis. Everything would be focused on real-world success and it was a huge benefit to all attendees.

One afternoon, the team for one of her students gathered around the conference room table to talk about next steps. The student, Brianna, would be a perfect candidate for the 18–21 program. Brianna was magical. She was creative, artistic and a total social butterfly. Everyone in her grade level knew and loved Brianna. She was center stage at the pep fest cheering the loudest. She was on the cheerleading team, the bowling team, and she rocked at adapted softball. Brianna loved life and had one of those contagious smiles that the whole world needs to see. Brianna's only struggle was her cognitive ability which created some challenges with her understanding and her academics. Despite these issues, she was flourishing. Giving her extra time at the 18–21 year old program would mean that she could flourish even more!

As the meeting began, team members went through introductions. Around the table were Brianna's mom Jen and dad Gerald, a general education teacher, an administrator, and our SPED teacher who served as both special education teacher and case manager.

"Okay, now that we've introduced ourselves, let's dive in to the meeting-" began Ms. Xiong.

"Oh, well this will be a short meeting," Gerald said. "We already have a plan for after high school."

"Oh... um... Great!" Ms. Xiong stumbled, "I had some ideas in mind too..."

DOI: 10.4324/9781003364443-8

"Well, not to worry," Gerald chimed in, "We have our application in at Briar Bend University to take after her old man! It's my alma mater."

Brianna's mom Jen clasped her hands on the table. She seemed to be studying her fingernails. She said nothing.

"Okay…" Ms. Xiong had to think fast. Jumping right into college would be way too much for Brianna at this point in her life. She would be clobbered by the rigor of the work and she wouldn't have the independence to navigate campus. How could she help Gerald understand this without squashing his dream for his daughter? College isn't out of the question, but giving Brianna more time and more support would help her first. She would have to learn a lot of self-advocacy skills to make it in that academic environment.

"Well I actually called the team together today to talk about an opportunity which might be a great fit for Brianna. Our district can offer Brianna a little more time to prepare for adult life before she moves on to college or whatever comes next. We have a program which focuses on life skills, independent living, and job preparation. Brianna would be a perfect fit!"

"Yes!" Jen spoke up instantly. "That sounds perfect for her!"

"Well, what about college… I want her to be able to get a good job and she needs an education," replied Gerald.

"The great thing about Brianna is that she has a lot of skills which will set her up for success at a job in the future. She's friendly, social, and she will be able to manage a job which involves regular routines she can learn. If she attends the 18–21 year old program, they will help with this. I could also talk with them about having Brianna try a college class while she is attending the program so that we can see how she handles it in a supported environment." Ms. Xiong was thinking on her feet. She knew she needed to lovingly guide the family toward the 18–21 year old program, but she also wanted to listen and be a good collaborator. At this moment, she realized she should have brought up the program much earlier in Brianna's education. She could have been preparing them all along so that they didn't feel they had to go out on their own and set up the college possibility. In the future, she would definitely lay the groundwork for future planning earlier in her conversations with families so there would be no surprises.

"Okay, I can see how that would be helpful…" Gerald tentatively replied.

"I think it would be great to see what Brianna says about all this. I sent her a pass to come and join us and she should be here any minute."

Moments later, Brianna entered the room with a huge smile and greeted her parents with a tight, squeezy hug. The atmosphere in the room turned to sunshine in Brianna's presence and there were smiles all around. Gerald explained the conversation they had been having about life after high school. Brianna expressed that she just wished she could stay at high school forever.

"I just want to stay with my friends. I'm sad about graduation," Brianna said.

"Okay, that's all I needed to hear," Gerald said. "Let's go for the school program first, and we can always try for the college thing down the road. I'm assuming some of Bri's friends are doing the program too?"

"Oh yes," Ms. Xiong said, "They will be learning all about the 'joys of adulting' together!"

Everyone around the circle shared a chuckle. In the end, Brianna was very successful in life. She stayed at the transition program until she turned 21 and transitioned into a job as an assistant manager at a local bakery. She was well-loved by the community and her colleagues, and her parents were thrilled. They learned that success looked a little different for Brianna than the life they had envisioned, and in actuality, things turned out better than expected!

As parents, we all have different hopes and dreams for our children. For some, this has to do with career success or earning potential. For others, like Gerald, this relates to following in the footsteps toward success which worked for us. I must admit that I would LOVE it if one of my children became a special education teacher because I love the work so very much. However, if there is one thing I've learned about parenting, it's that imposing my will on my children often blows up in my face and often, my best course of action is to sit back and watch as they learn to make their own decisions. It is healthy and important for them to carve out their own paths and make their own decisions as much as possible. The self-determination we discussed in past chapters can only come to fruition if we let our children find their way through trial and error at times.

> The road to success is rarely a nice straight line. We can support our children through the twists, turns, speed bumps, potholes, and road-blocks with our consistent presence and love.

The road to success is rarely a nice straight line. We can support our children through the twists, turns, speed bumps, potholes, and roadblocks with our consistent presence and love.

As our children develop and find their identity, there is one enemy which will drive us to frustration and stress as parents: perfectionism. We must realize that life just isn't perfect, that our children will make mistakes and confound us at times, and that success may look quite different than what we initially envisioned for them. In my world, success for my own children and for my students means that they build a life in which they are content, satisfied, and as independent as possible. This chapter will help us redefine success, let go of perfection and other unproductive patterns of thought, and develop the tools to help our children truly thrive.

Key Themes

♦ Life will never be perfect, but it can be pretty great: Expecting perfection is unhelpful in the parenting journey and the more you can 'let things go,' the happier you'll be.
♦ Focus on your own strengths as a parent and capitalize on them. Don't expect yourself to be perfect and realize that you will make mistakes as part of the process.
♦ Your hopes and dreams for your child will change over and over again. Create a new definition of 'success' in your mind based on progress, not perfection.
♦ Preserving your loving relationship with your child eclipses all other aspects of your role as a parent. It is key to take the pressure off of yourself at times and just enjoy each other.
♦ There is no such thing as a 'perfect' parent or child, so let go of unreasonable expectations for yourself or your child.
♦ Celebrations are important and should focus on even the smallest 'wins' in the life of your child.
♦ Flexibility is not optional if you want to enjoy your life as a parent.

Let Go of Perfection

Throughout my life, I have always tended toward perfectionism. I'm an achiever. I like to get the job done and get it done well. I always felt rather accomplished in my work and could execute the demands of life with excellence. When I became a mother, my sense of accomplishment came to a screeching halt. Suddenly I held a young life in my hands. A young life who was screaming, wriggling, and needed a diaper change. It was terrifying and overwhelming. I found myself remiss to be the 'perfect' mom I wanted to be and entered into survival mode rather quickly. Over time, I figured it out and found a healthy rhythm of parenting and rest, but it definitely took some time. The most important lesson I learned was that there is no such thing as 'achievement' when it comes to our kids. There is no trophy for doing parenting 'right' and you can't win at it. The concept of 'perfect' must be tossed out the window. The journey toward *lasting joy* as a parent begins with one simple rule: Let. Go. Of. Perfection. Wake up every morning ready to give it your best and expect things to be messy at times. Make plans for yourself and your child and

> The journey toward lasting joy as a parent begins with one simple rule: Let. Go. Of. Perfection.

then hold them very loosely. Stay open to what life brings you with the knowledge that you can surmount any challenge which comes your way.

Your child is a human being. You love your child, you empower your child, you inspire your child, and often you will discover that their thoughts and actions make absolutely no sense to you. Your best laid parenting plans may blow up in your face at times. In these moments, the best you may be able to offer to yourself is, 'Well, at least I tried.' I implore you to keep your sense of humor as you ride the parenting roller coaster.

Parenting is a deeply personal act which is unique to each individual. You bring your own ideas, style, and personality to the table, and that's part of the beauty of parenting. Don't get hung up on whether you are doing it 'right' or 'wrong,' because things just aren't concrete, no matter how frustrating this can be at times. Focus on good things you see in your child. Infuse your life with laughter and love, letting go of stringent rules which try to create the 'perfect' home and child.

YOU Are Strong!

Over my years as a special educator and a mother, there has been a lot of talk about the importance of focusing on a child's strengths and incorporating them in our parenting and teaching. This seems to be a common sense approach to helping our children feel capable and valued both at home and at school. The problem? While there is plenty of talk about strengths-based practice, we continue to function from a deficit model in special education.

> It is imperative that we remember that we have so much to offer our children, and our loving presence is the most important asset we have to give.

This can trickle over into a focus on problems rather than strengths as we support our children in the home setting. The school system requires proof that a student isn't succeeding and too often, their strengths fall by the wayside, eclipsed by their many difficulties as they enter special education services. See Chapter 1 for activities and suggestions to help you highlight your child's strengths throughout the educational process.

Just as we may place too much emphasis on deficits in children, the same can happen for us as parents. At times, the difficulties of our tasks as parents can cause us to feel inadequate. We forget the many strengths we possess and may neglect to offer them to our children. I know that I have found myself in a 'downward spiral' at times, especially when my child seems to be struggling and there is nothing I can do to help, or when I feel ineffective with a student I care about very deeply. In these moments, it is key that I encourage myself, remember my strengths, and stand on past successes to rekindle my joy. It is imperative that we remember that we have so much to offer our children, and our loving presence is the most important asset we have to give. Tapping into our own strength as parents may offer the boost we need to enjoy our children and our life experiences together.

> Tapping into our own strengths as parents may offer the boost we need to enjoy our children and our life experiences together.

I don't know about you, but one of the most difficult questions I face in life is "What are your strengths?" I remember back in the days when I was preparing for a job interview, I always seemed to draw a blank at this question. When I think about this now, it makes me realize why I was so unsure of myself and so insecure. Today I have learned to identify and stand in my strengths as a person and a parent. I celebrate what I'm good at and I hope you learn to do the same! You may begin by answering simple questions such as:

- ◆ What skills or tasks come easily to you?
- ◆ What do you like most about yourself?
- ◆ What are your best characteristics?
- ◆ What are you good at?

You may find it helpful to write down your responses to these questions as an informal journaling exercise. Take the time to seek out and examine even your most subtle positive attributes.

My Strengths as a Parent

Positive Attributes:

Five characteristics which help me parent include:

1. _____
2. _____
3. _____
4. _____
5. _____

Hope-Giving Beliefs:

I believe I can share hope with my child by:

_____

_____

_____

_____

Celebrations:

If times get tough, I can stand on successes from the past such as:

_____

_____

_____

_____

Lasting Rewards:

My strengths may have a positive an impact on my child in the future in the following ways:

_____

_____

_____

_____

Stand on your successes and let them be a beacon of hope for you in times of challenge. See Activity 23 for an activity entitled "My Strengths as a Parent" that you can complete for yourself in order to identify and utilize their positive attributes. Hang onto this document and celebrate who you are. You have much to offer, and you will be happier in life if you believe in your own capability and competence!

Share Your Story

As parents, it may be natural to experience a sense of pressure to portray ourselves as infallible and even perfect in the eyes of our children. As a mom, I know that I desperately want to set a good example for the watchful eyes of my two little ones. In reality, it helps us to remember that our children may learn from our flubs and our mistakes just as much as they may learn from our positive example. We are not robots and as we live in this world as imperfect people, there will most certainly be times when our children observe us in moments of struggle, difficulty, and even exasperation. Every interaction will not be sunshine and rainbows. Every parental decision will not be impeccably executed and that's okay! What is important is that we preserve our lasting positive relationships with our children through consistent love, communication, and at times, an expression of our own humility.

The knowledge that my children are always watching motivates me to approach them with warmth, caring, and consistency. Our children are tremendously perceptive. They can sense when we are doing our best, even when we aren't the perfect parents. Our love for them shines through in small acts every day, whether we are scrambling eggs, buying new socks, or driving them to an important appointment. When things do go awry and our human frailty shines through, we have the chance to repair the relationship quickly and return to that place of peaceful harmony through a renewed commitment to a warm and caring approach.

As parents, we all have stories of our own from the trials and challenges of growing up. We have a rich personal history of successes and mistakes which can offer our children valuable

> We have a rich personal history of successes and mistakes which can offer our children valuable lessons.

lessons. One of the best ways we can share our common humanity with our children is to offer them our stories. This can be a strategic and purposeful parenting tool, and when executed well, it can be extremely powerful. While our children certainly need to see us as wise sources of guidance in their lives, they also may benefit from seeing us as lifelong learners who are still developing and growing every day.

One of my favorite tools for quick and easy connection and instruction with my children is something I call 'strategic self-disclosure' or sharing my stories. I maintain the practice of selecting pivotal experiences to share in order to help my children understand their own lives. For example, I struggled to figure out where I would 'fit' during the transition from elementary school to middle school. One of my closest friends moved away to another state and I found myself struggling to find connection. To make matters worse, I found that none of my friends had been scheduled during my lunch period and I didn't know who I would sit with to eat lunch. To my middle school self, this seemed devastating. When one of my own children was struggling with a similar issue, I shared this story to help explain that in the long run, it all worked out. Looking back I can chuckle at the awkward challenges of middle school, and I can assure young people everywhere that it most certainly gets better. I offered this story to my children to invite them to open up about their own lunchroom difficulties. This created an avenue for a lovely conversation. It also helped my children to understand that many of their struggles are common across the human experience. Dr. Kristin Neff, prolific researcher on the concept of self-compassion, purports that one of the key elements of self-compassion is a recognition that many struggles are shared as a part of our common humanity (Germer and Neff, 2013). This beautiful concept may offer comfort to our children as we share our stories with them.

> In my experience, the more 'real' I am able to be, the more open, honest, and communicative my children will be in return.

In my experience, the more 'real' I am able to be, the more open, honest, and engaged my children will be in return. When you begin to share information about who you are and your personal life, your children begin to see you as real people with your own difficulties and struggles. We model resilience and self-efficacy through our stories. We also model our okay-ness with our own human imperfection. So how can you practice strategic sharing to improve outcomes and deepen connection with your children? Consider the following tips when choosing to share your stories:

- ◆ Determine your boundaries: When selecting personal information to share, remember that you are the parent, not a friend, and it is important to filter out information which may be too much for your child. Over-sharing may make them uncomfortable and may work against your intentions. Wisdom is necessary to ensure that the information you share is instructive and understandable for your children, without including details which may be unnecessary or detrimental to them.

- ◆ Identify common difficulties: Plan the stories you plan to share based on specific difficulties you are seeing in your child. Think of a story you might share if your child feels upset with a friend. Maybe there was a time you over-came an academic obstacle. Think about a story you could share if your child makes a mistake and feels remorseful or stressed. Make sure the story you choose to share matches your child's situation, or you may find that they don't make the connection and benefit from the instructive anecdote.

- ◆ Build safety and trust: Establish and uphold the expecta-tion that your home is a space of safety and trust. As you share your stories, expect that your children will learn that your home is a safe space for open lines of commu-nication and sharing. By sharing your experiences, you are showing your children that you trust them enough to hold space for your stories. This is a beautiful way to con-vey a sense of trust. Children thrive when they receive the message: I believe that you are becoming a trustworthy,

Stories to Share

Complete the following with short stories from your personal life that you can share with your child. Focus on situations in which you struggled or made mistakes but were able to overcome them. This shows your child that you are real, modeling perseverance and a growth mindset:

A time I set and achieved an important goal:	
A time I made a mistake and was able to make it right.	
A time when I felt a strong, overwhelming emotion and I handled it.	
A time when I was upset with someone and we made up.	
A time someone was upset with me and I made it right.	

dependable person. Sharing our stories offers them this implicit message.

◆ Invite reciprocal sharing: As you share your stories, invite your child to share in return. The more we can get our children talking about their experiences, struggles, and difficulties, the more we can put ourselves in their shoes and help them solve problems before they start. As children grow into adolescence, there is a natural developmental tendency for them to differentiate from their parents by pulling away and establishing their own identities (Gilbertson, 2014). This process is necessary, but it does not mean that open communication needs to stop. Reciprocal sharing can help keep critical connections going to help young people navigate the challenges and pressures of their adolescent years with the support of their parents.

When we share our stories with our children, we offer them the unspoken message, "This is who I am, and I want to know who you are." This can help to tear down walls which may grow between parents and children, as they express common learning experiences and shared humanity. So, I encourage you to open up, share about your struggles and imperfections, and you will be leveraging them to help your child! Activity 24 provides an activity you can complete to plan for the stories you will share with your child to help support this process. Enjoy!

Progress, Not Perfection

High personal standards? Good.
Expecting great things from your child? Fabulous.
A staunch adherence to perfection at all costs? Not so great.
Unrealistic expectations for your child's achievement? Very not so great.

Perfectionists struggle in the world of parenting, particularly when a child has special needs. Perfectionistic parents may be far more vulnerable to both emotional distress and physical health problems which can impede their overall functioning and their ability to provide what their child needs from them (Sirois and Molnar, 2020). Parenting a child with special needs is a complex, difficult, and unpredictable task, any way you slice it. Perfectionism works against parents, and those who thrive find a way to hold themselves to a high set of standards without burning themselves out. Yet, how does one who has high personal standards let go of the unreasonable ideal of perfection? If we truly love our children, shouldn't we strive to be perfect for them? Absolutely not. Rather, I suggest a relentless focus on progress and regular celebration of the small successes which happen all the time in the beautiful little microcosm of a family.

It is completely natural to want our children to succeed. We have a vision for the amazing little people we want them to become. When we don't see the gains and growth we hope for, we too easily blame ourselves or find ourselves feeling defeated. At times we hope to accomplish goals which turn out to be unattainable or more long term than we realized, either for ourselves or for our child. We can combat the stress this may cause by fixing our eyes on the progress our child is making. Celebrate every small win, every little smile, every adjustment you make that helps, every new learning experience. Your child is growing every day and so are you. If you see life as a test to pass or a game to win, you will falter and struggle. If you see life as a learning experience and an opportunity for ongoing development, you will find yourself inspired.

> Celebrate every small win, every little smile, every adjustment you make that helps, every new learning experience.

As parents, it can be easy to feel bogged down by the many needs and pressures involved in our role. One of the most stressful endeavors of my life has been raising my two children, and I believe this hails from the fact that we have a deep, vested interest in their success. We love our children so deeply; we want them to find a path of happiness, strength, and contribution to the world around them. We want them to feel fulfilled and satisfied throughout their lives, and at times, it can seem as if they are heading in the wrong direction. We will inevitably experience a sense of powerlessness which can be overwhelming when it comes to the success of our children. Here it helps to reflect on what we can control, which is our ability to infuse their lives with a focus on their strengths and on what is going well.

How might you return to a focus on what is going well? I believe a powerful tool you might embrace in your family is that of celebration. Celebration is highly unique to each culture, family, and individual. It is a nearly universal part of the human experience, and different forms of celebration can be found across the globe in various forms (Gopalkrishnan, 2019). Essentially, celebration is important, and it can be woven into the lifestyle of your family to create a happier, healthier home experience. Weaving celebration into my classroom practice with intention is something which has had a powerful impact on students, and my hope is that this helps your child in the home setting as well.

Perhaps you already adhere to some celebration practices in your usual routines. In my family, we enjoy habitual celebrations such as birthday dinners and specific holidays. We also practice less formal celebration routines such as Friday night pizza or a picnic dinner in the park on the last day of the school year. Things may look quite different in your family, but no matter what, you may discover that you naturally involve celebration in regular practice without fully realizing it. As you consider possibilities to bring even more celebration into your home, Activity 25 provides a 'Celebration Plan' to help you lay out the ways you might recognize accomplishments both big and small in your family. As you complete the plan, you may consider identifying progress in many different forms in order to recognize achievements. Examples may include:

- ◆ Your family makes it through a challenging transition such as moving to a new home or city.
- ◆ A member of the family accomplishes a personal goal such as completing a phase of their education or engaging in a new and challenging task.
- ◆ Your children finish up another year of school with all of its ups and downs.

- ◆ To commemorate a special date unique to your family such as the date you brought home a new pet.
- ◆ Even a simple accomplishment such as remembering to brush teeth at bedtime every evening for a week can be a cause for celebration!

Realize that there is ALWAYS something to celebrate if you examine situations carefully enough. Note that the intention of celebration is not necessarily to incentivize your child or children. It is not meant to provide a 'carrot on a stick' to motivate their actions. Rather, the celebration is intended to be a natural and positive part of the family climate to set the stage for greater warmth and joy overall. Using celebration as an incentive may actually cause them to become less desirable because they become attached to something undesirable or off-putting. Celebrate the wins simply because they happened, rather than using the celebration to cause them to happen.

You may also reflect on your own accomplishments as a parent and celebrate them as well. Did you finish a task you were dreading? Celebrate. Did you connect with your child on a new level? Celebrate. Did you get out of bed this morning and show up for your kids? Celebrate! Sometimes, we take what we can get! As you think about how you can celebrate yourself, plan to offer yourself the things which make you happy and bring you the most joy. For some, this means tangible rewards such as a special treat or activity. For others, this means intangible rewards such as taking extra time to rest and relax. Finding connection and joining with other parents to celebrate your small wins (even if that small win is survival at times), can be a life-giving practice which can build you up to bring your best to your family. Activity 7 also includes an area for you to reflect on how you plan to celebrate yourself as a parent when you have the chance. Remember, we must not neglect our own needs in favor of the needs of our children or family, or we will most certainly burn out. So, here you go: I give you full permission to take the time to celebrate YOU, a parent who is bringing their best each day!

Family Celebration Plan

Use this form to remind yourself to celebrate PROGRESS at regular intervals in your family. Remember, strive for progress, not perfection!

Circle the times in the year when you plan to celebrate progress:

Start of the school year	End of the school year	Before a break from school	After a break from school
Completely at random- Surprise!	Whenever you have a small win	When a family member reaches a goal	When you observe acts of kindness
Special holidays or dates	Birthdays and anniversaries	After a difficult event	Kicking off a new season

Four ways I might celebrate MYSELF as a parent:

Ways to treat myself (intangible)	
Ways to treat myself (tangible)	
Friends to celebrate with:	
Ways to celebrate with other parents	

Flexibility: Your Saving Grace!

Over the years, I have noticed that my happiest parent friends are also the most flexible. For the sake of your own joy and wholeness in your life as a parent, I suggest you learn to be flexible too. Being flexible can be absolutely terrifying. For those of us who enjoy feeling in control, it can feel like falling without a parachute at first. Opening our minds and hearts and souls to the flow of the day isn't comfortable at first, and in fact, some find it terrifying. The underlying need for control can drive us into some pretty unproductive strategies as parents. It can cause us to make up unnecessary rules, engage in silly power struggles, and cling to schedules or plans which just don't suit our child's needs. The desire to control the world around us is often driven by fear of what will happen if we loosen up and let go of the reins. So I encourage you to be fearless, loosen your grip on life, and see what happens. Most often your children will surprise you in delightful ways when you loosen your tight grip and choose to enjoy them for who they are.

> Expect the unexpected, go with the flow, and know that you will rise to any challenge life can throw at you!

In my years and years in special education, and as a parent for that matter, I can't recall a single day which unfolded entirely according to plan. The need for flexibility is one of the only guarantees I can think of in any kind of interaction with young people. Flexibility is not an option if we want to stay happy, and it's as simple as that. Expect the unexpected, go with the flow, and know that you will rise to any challenge life can throw at you!

Confidence and flexibility go hand in hand. Believe in yourself! You can manage whatever comes your way through flexibility, not perfectionism. Flexibility is key in deepening your connection with your child and making sure their needs are being met. Children need parents who are able to work with their needs 'in the moment' and adjust plans accordingly. We can approach our lives as parents with the knowledge that nothing is set in stone and adjusting in the moment is an unavoidable part of the role. This means that we sometimes get to change the tire as the car speeds down the road – lucky us! However, if we see parenting as an adventure and realize that at times we are just along for the ride, we can better enjoy the journey. We can be flexible and relational parents who leave space for tangential conversations, following our children down the 'rabbit hole,' showing our children that we care about their interests and needs more than the predetermined plan for the day or our own distractions.

> As our children change, so must our parenting and our approaches. It's just the nature of life as a parent.

Perfectionism breeds rigidity. Why? Because in order to be 'perfect,' things need to fit within the tidy little boxes we have envisioned for our practice. Your child is changing every single day. They are growing, learning, developing, and shaping themselves into the person they want to be. One day, you may wake up and feel that a stranger is living in your home. This has definitely happened to me as my youngster became a teenager seemingly overnight. As our children change, so must our parenting and our approaches. It's just the nature of life as a parent. Conclusion? Purposefully choose the flexible response whenever you can. You may just find this to be a lifesaver in your relationship with your child. See Table 5.1 for examples of rigid vs. flexible responses.

Just as you are flexible and gracious to your child, there are many benefits to offering this same flexibility to yourself! There was a time in my parenting life when I was plagued by one of the most dangerous and exhausting habits a human being can face: Ruminating. I was the queen of all ruminators, and I obsessed over every little thing, especially my own actions and potential mistakes. I would replay every word I spoke after even simple conversations with school or other family members and think things like, 'I wish I wouldn't have said that,' or 'I should have said _____

> Just as you are flexible and gracious to your child, there are many benefits to offering this same flexibility to yourself!

TABLE 5.1 Examples of Rigid vs. Flexible Responses

Situation	Rigid Response (Impairs Relationships)	Flexible Response (Fosters Relationships)
Your child forgets their backpack at home with all of their belongings for the day.	Tell them to figure it out on their own or punish them for their forgetfulness.	Run their backpack to school if possible and make a proactive plan for the future so this doesn't happen again.
Your child is struggling to wake up on time in the morning and is consistently causing the family to run late.	Give them consequences like extra chores or removing preferred items.	Discuss the problem and make a plan to help your child get better sleep. Get them an alarm clock of their own to facilitate independence.
Your child is obsessed with a high-interest topic and won't talk about anything else.	Tell your child that they aren't allowed to talk about that topic anymore.	Listen to your child, but also express that you would like to chat about other things as well.
Your child won't stop starting conflicts with a sibling over small issues.	Give them consequences for starting issues. Keep the siblings apart at all times.	Invite your children to talk things out with your help. Arrive at compromises over small issues. Model tolerance, flexibility, and love.

instead.' If my child had a tough day or there was a negative incident, I would overthink my part in the chain of events looking for where I might be to blame. It was as if I was seeking out my own imperfections and over-analyzing them.

If you identify with this habit, I beg of you to please STOP! There is a vast difference between reflection and rumination. Reflection is a healthy practice which invites you to think about what went well and what went not-so-great so that you can improve in the future. All of us have room for growth. Rumination is an unhealthy indulgence which focuses on the negative, creates stress, and leads to broken relationships. So please, keep on reflecting, keep growing, but avoid ruminating. A dear friend of mine used to say, "If you are beating yourself up, put down the bat and pick up a feather!"

Set up Family Standards

For many years of my life, I had no idea who I was or what I believed. My teaching career started very young, and in my early 1920s, I had just as much to learn about myself as I did about my students. Then, at 27, I became a mom, adding another element to my identity and yet, deepening the sense of uncertainty about the person I wanted to be. As I worked on carving out my true adult identity as a mom, I found myself struggling to trust myself and my ability to be the best I could be for myself and my child. I knew that confidence in life was key, but I was often plagued by self-doubt after choosing a course of action. There were also plenty of mistakes along the way, which is a natural part of life, but which only served to deepen my lack of self-trust. That unproductive perfectionism would pop up no matter how much I tried to keep a lid on it.

Today, I have learned to trust myself as a parent, standing on the fact that I have the skills to make good decisions for my children and that I can equip them to make good decisions on their own. You will be much more relaxed and confident in your life if you learn to trust in your ability to make sound decisions for your children. Self-trust and confidence are choices you can make. You can decide today to put aside self-doubt and stand on who you are and what you believe with the deep faith that you are doing what is right for your child. After making a decision, cast aside the temptation to question yourself and move forward based on the course of action you have chosen. You will stop wasting energy on useless thoughts, and you will be happier as a parent.

> You can decide today to put aside self-doubt and stand on who you are and what you believe with the deep faith that you are doing what is right for your child.

One proactive step you can take now to improve your decision-making skills is to define your standards. A standard is a level of quality or achievement that is considered acceptable or desirable (Merriam-Webster, 2021). A set of clear, non-negotiable standards were the missing piece of the puzzle for me when I was a young parent. As I grew in my sense of self, I developed a clear understanding of my personal guidelines and this helped me tremendously. You operate from your own set of standards for life without even realizing it. Taking the time to specify your standards in different areas may help with letting go of perfectionism, as you develop your own sense of what is right and wrong based on your personal ethics. You can base your life on these simple principles and then exercise flexibility with everything else. Standards may be written as 'I statements' which function as commitments to oneself. Examples may include:

- ◆ I make sure my children have their basic needs met daily.
- ◆ I support my child's education and make it a priority.
- ◆ I take care of myself and manage my stress to be a healthier parent.

Once you identify a clear set of personal standards, you might utilize them to keep life simple. The ultimate result may be less stress and more joy in general. As you set your standards, focus on your heart of love for your child and your commitment to bring them your best each day!

Just as you benefit from this practice, your family as a whole may also set their own standards to help you come together based on what you believe. Too often, we are tossed around by life, letting the actions of others or unexpected circumstances dictate our course of action and decisions. We can help our children define who they are and how they will set their own priorities by inviting them to participate in creating a set of family standards. An example may be, we spend time together without our phones to distract us at least once per day. Another example may be, we are kind to each other and we support each other. Activity 26 offers an activity entitled 'Our Family Standards' which may be used to help your family define your own basic rules or guidelines for living. This can be so powerful as your children move into the later years of their teenage years and prepare to transition to adulthood. Basic standards plant the seeds which will help them grow into who they are.

Our Family Standards

Discuss the standards and values you share as a family in each area. If you need to make a decision or you are struggling, come back to your standards.

Area	Our Beliefs and Standards
The way we treat each other.	
The way we treat other people.	
The way we take care of ourselves.	
The way we spend our time and set priorities.	
The way we treat teachers and people in charge.	
The importance of education/schoolwork.	
Jobs and the importance of work.	

Conclusion

Let this chapter be a love letter to our imperfect, messy, unpredictable role as parents. Raising little people is rarely boring, and you will learn to live life on your toes, especially as you help your child make the most out of their experience in special education. Trust yourself and believe in your ability to manage anything that comes your way. Make every effort to enjoy the journey. Let go of the perfectionist mindset and celebrate progress instead. Be who you are and bring your authentic self to your children, sharing your own stories of challenges and difficulties. There is no absolute 'right way' to do this job. There are too many variables involved, and the parents who excel are flexible and find a way to celebrate even the smallest 'wins' with their children. Set up standards for yourself and your family, and aside from these non-negotiable principles, stay flexible along the way.

As you strive to be a present, loving parent, this is a beautiful, meaningful gift you get to give to society and your child. The very fact that you are reading this book means that you are trying your very best. Being a parent does not mean that you have to put on a cape and become a superhero overnight. You are human. This means you have a lot to offer, but it also means there are limits to what you have to give. Show up for your child, keep doing all that you can, and everything else falls into place, even when things get messy. Remember the personal strengths you bring to your parenting and reflect on how you can bring these into your interactions with your child. If you find yourself struggling, rest assured that things are usually better than you think and return to the things you love about your amazing, unique, sometimes mysterious child! Our next chapter will walk you into the dark, murky swamp of behavioral challenges and will offer you a bright lantern to find your path in the darkness of difficulty.

Chapter 5 Simple Snapshot

◆ Value progress over perfection – both for yourself and your child. There is no such thing as 'perfect' anyway.
◆ Identify and utilize your own strengths when it comes to your parenting. You will enjoy the experience much more.
◆ Share your story and include times when you made mistakes and overcame challenges. Be real with your child about the messiness of life.
◆ Redefine the meaning of 'success' and celebrate even the smallest wins in your family. Make celebrations a regular part of the fabric of your family.
◆ Flexibility is not optional if you want to enjoy life as a parent – expect the unexpected!
◆ Develop a set of 'family standards' which define what is important to all members and stick to them with dedication. Keep everything else flexible.

Chapter 5 Reflection Questions

Use the following questions to reflect on what you have learned in the chapter. You may choose to journal about them or discuss them with a partner or small group to gain further insights.

1. What are some areas in which you struggle with perfectionism? How has this helped or hindered you?
2. What are some ways you might celebrate progress rather than perfection? How might celebration help your child?
3. How might it help you to identify your own strengths as a parent? How might this help you enjoy your family life more?
4. What are some instructive stories you could share with your child right now to help demonstrate problem-solving and resilience?

5. What are some standards you hold for yourself which might also help your family? How might 'family standards' help guide your decision-making?
6. How do you define 'success'? What are your ultimate hopes and dreams for your child?

References

Germer, C.K. & Neff, K.D. (2013). Self-compassion in clinical practice: Self-compassion. *Journal of Clinical Psychology*, vol. 69, no. 8, pp. 856–867, doi:10.1002/jclp.22021.

Gilbertson, T. (2014). *Differentiation: 'Normal' Estrangement from Parents?* Retrieved September 30, 2022 from https://tinagilbertson.com/differentiation/.

Gopalkrishnan, N. (2019). Cultural competence and beyond: Working across cultures in culturally dynamic partnerships. *The International Journal of Community and Social Development*, vol. 1, no. 1, pp. 28–41, doi:10.1177/2516602619826712.

Merriam-Webster. 2021. Standard. In *Merriam-Webster.com*. Retrieved October 28, 2021, from https://www.merriam-webster.com/dictionary/standard.

Sirois, Fuschia M. & Molnar, Danielle S. (2016). *Perfectionism, health, and well-being*. Cham, CH: Springer International Publishing.

6

Thriving through Challenges

David Forrest became a single parent when his daughter AJ was in 4th grade. He loved being a dad and always had a lot of fun with AJ. She had a big, huge personality, and you always knew when AJ was in the room. She loved to communicate and would talk at length about her area of special interest: Cats. AJ knew the history of the domestic housecat back to the days of ancient Egypt. She knew every species of cat in the wild kingdom. She was a walking cat encyclopedia, and the trouble was, sometimes people didn't want to learn cat trivia or listen to a lecture on the role of cats in the farmsteads of the early 1800s. AJ had a big, loud voice, a boisterous personality, and an infectious smile.

When AJ was younger, the school had determined that she had a need for special education services in the area of autism spectrum disorder and her pediatrician agreed. AJ struggled with perspective-taking, sensory processing and social interaction. David could see the issues described by the school and the doctor, and at times, AJ's struggles led to outbursts at home. She would raise her voice and even damage property when she was overwhelmed. Most often, her worst struggles were at bedtime when she didn't want to turn off her cat Youtube videos and go to sleep. It was getting to the point that it took an hour to persuade AJ to transition to bedtime, and David was becoming exhausted.

David decided to ask AJ's case manager for any ideas or suggestions to help with the bedtime issues. He sent her an email requesting help with the transition time. The case manager responded with the following message:

Greetings,

Thanks for your question. At school, we find that AJ struggles most when she is hungry, so you might consider a small bedtime snack to help her put down the Youtube videos and to stabilize her mood. We also use a timer to show AJ how much time she has left before a transition and it really seems to help. At home you could set a timer on your microwave or use a simple kitchen timer. I'm so glad you reached out and that you are helping AJ get enough sleep. We will keep working on transitions here at school and I will let you know if I come up with any more ideas to help. Have a great day.

David was skeptical that a snack and a timer would actually help, but he decided to give it a try. He set a timer 30 minutes before bedtime to give AJ

DOI: 10.4324/9781003364443-9

plenty of notice. When the timer beeped, he offered AJ her favorite snack –
string cheese – and AJ's eyes lit up.
    "Really dad? Can I have two?"
    "Sure why not. Then it's time to brush those teeth and hop into bed. Deal?"
David smiled.
    "DEAL!" AJ replied, turning off her device and bounding toward the fridge.
    David was pleasantly surprised by the success of these easy strategies. After
a few nights, the novelty wore off and AJ started to balk at bedtime a bit, but she
continued to follow the new routine. David sent a word of thanks to AJ's case
manager and sighed a breath of relief. He planned to continue to keep his eye
out for proactive approaches he could take with AJ to help her avoid outbursts
and to preserve his own peace.

Special education teachers consistently report dealing with student behavior to be among the most challenging issues they face daily (Scott, 2017). Thus, most have developed a full toolbox of interventions which work well with students. David's choice to reach out to school helped him tremendously, and the case manager was happy to share ideas. As a special educator, I love to share ideas to help parents navigate the murky waters of behavioral intervention. The more I can support parents, the better I am setting the stage for their child's success. Behavioral intervention can be highly unpredictable and emotionally charged. It can make or break relationships and lead to a peaceful household or a setting of stressful chaos. This chapter is designed to help you mitigate undesirable behavior to enjoy your parenting journey!

Every child on earth will engage in some type of behavior which confounds, frustrates, or bothers the adults in their lives. It's just part of the deal when we take on the role of parent. Supporting your child through behavioral difficulties may be likened to a rustic camping excursion. One may prepare diligently, packing resources for every potential issue and bringing state-of-the-art equipment and yet, this doesn't ensure smooth sailing. One may experience glorious sunsets, relaxing afternoons in a canoe, glowing bonfires, and comfy nights of fitful sleep. On the other hand, one may encounter thunderstorms, torrential rains, rampant insect attacks, extreme heat, freezing temperatures, and even bears. Even the most experienced camper may be unprepared for what is thrown their way. As parents, we must anticipate the unexpected, preparing our hearts and minds to weather

Key Themes

♦ All behavior is communication. Look for the hidden patterns and messages to be as proactive as possible.
♦ The underlying goal of behavioral intervention is to preserve a healthy relationship with your child.
♦ Inviting your child to identify the stimuli which lead to negative behaviors can help them grow self-management abilities.
♦ Maintaining your own healthy mindset is critical to your happiness as a parent.
♦ Taking your child's behavior personally can lead to greater emotional difficulty and stress for you as a parent.
♦ Undesirable behavior often occurs because your child does not understand the implied expectations in various contexts.
♦ Common unmet basic needs like hunger or fatigue can initiate negative behavior, and thus, healthy routines may prevent problems.

whatever challenges may come along. The outside forces at work have a tremendous impact on what happens in each interaction with our child, including the potential impact of their disability (Galvin, 2016). Striving for complete control is a futile exercise which will only exacerbate stress and lead you to exhaustion.

The simple solution? Parents must tend to their own health and wholeness (see Chapters 8–10 of this book). From this place, you may take on the attitude that no matter what may arise, love for your child will prevail. You can also learn and practice the mindsets and strategies included in this chapter. Keep in mind that some days will be better than others. To return to the camping analogy, there will be days of sunshine and days of torrential rain. No matter what happens, parents who strive to see the best in their child every day can better maintain their connection and enjoyment of the human being they are trying to raise.

Behavior Is Communication

Children are communicating all day long whether they are speaking or not. Their actions are often their expression of their truths, and much can be learned from careful observation of their interactions and patterns. As parents, we can help both ourselves and our child when we view their behavior as a message about what they need. 'Listening' and responding to the unspoken signals in a child's actions can mitigate conflict and power struggles (Greene, 2015). One rule I try to hold in my life, both as a parent and a special education teacher, is that I will not engage in power struggles. This can be incredibly difficult and at times I am nearly 'sucked in,' but I strive to stick to it. Rather than getting into 'battles' with my children or students, I follow these simple steps:

1. I state my expectation or direction clearly and simply. I try to be as concise as I can.
2. If my children or students argue, negotiate, or resist, I PAUSE. I wait and say nothing.
3. If my child or student continues to resist, I kindly and gently restate the simple expectation or direction using the same words. I usually add a warm smile.
4. Nearly every time, my child or student realizes they won't get anywhere and they follow the expectation or direction.
5. I reflect on possible unmet needs which might be causing their resistance so I can be proactive next time. What is the underlying communication?

In addition to power struggles, nothing will create frustration faster for both you and your child than trying to 'punish' or 'assign consequences' to change behavior when the unmet need in the child remains. Perhaps your child needs instruction in a particular skill area. Perhaps there is a missing resource your child needs in a physical or emotional sense. Teaching the skill or meeting the need can result in lasting positive changes. While punishment and consequences may have been a part of your upbringing, these won't be effective if your child doesn't have the skills or tools to meet the demands. The behavior is saying something or serving the child in some way.

> While punishment and consequences may have been a part of your upbringing, these won't be effective if your child doesn't have the skills or tools to meet the demands.

In special education, one of the assessments we utilize when students struggle with their behavior is called a 'functional behavior assessment.' In this kind of assessment, we explore how the undesirable behavior may be serving the child. We collect 'snapshots' each time a negative behavior occurs looking for what happened immediately before and after. Then, we analyze the 'snapshots' for patterns, seeking to identify areas in which

TABLE 6.1 Potential functions or purposes behind undesirable behavior with ideas to prevent future issues, teach new skills and reinforce positive choices.

Possible Function	Prevent	Teach	Reinforce
Attention	Provide attention when your child engages in appropriate behaviors on a consistent and frequent schedule.	Instruct your child in ways to ask for attention in prosocial ways (e.g., "Take a look at this.")	When your child makes an appropriate request for attention, provide it immediately.
Access to a desired activity or item	Set up clear expectations regarding how your child can access a preferred item or activity. If needed, use a timer to indicate when your child will have access to the desired activity or item.	Instruct your child in ways to ask for the desired item or activity in a prosocial way. You may even teach your child how to set timers for themselves to keep track of the time.	Provide your child with access to the activity or item immediately when they ask for it in an appropriate way and at the right time. Set up opportunities in which your child is likely to succeed in making the request.
Escape	Set up predictable routines within activities which allow your child to make choices. For example, if you are trying to invite them to help with household tasks, ask, "Would you rather do the dishes or vacuum?"	Instruct your child to ask for a break in a prosocial way rather than engaging in escape behaviors when they are engaging in undesirable tasks. Allow breaks immediately and then gradually increase time intervals between them to build your child's stamina.	Create routines for your child as much as possible. Help them know when to expect transitions such as leaving for school in the morning, mealtimes, and bedtime. When they follow the routines well, provide praise and encourage independence.

we might enact three steps to reduce challenging behavior: First, prevent the occurrences of the behavior by adjusting the environment to support the student; second, teach the student skills which appear to be missing; and finally, reinforce appropriate replacement skills whenever they occur (Chazin and Ledford, 2016). You can follow a similar approach at home. Pay attention to your child's patterns. What happens before and after a negative behavior? Then, think about the function the behavior may be serving for your child. How could you meet the need before they act out in order to try to meet it on their own? Table 6.1 provides further details and ideas on how this may take place.

Preserving Relationships

From the moment we begin our journey with our child, we enter into a process called 'Attachment.' Attachment theory states that an infant's early caregiving experiences build the foundation for how human beings see themselves and others, and that this persists throughout the child's development (Schröder et al., 2019). This means that if the child experiences love, warmth, and nurturing, they may be better able to connect with others throughout life. If the child experiences rejection or neglect, they may struggle with their sense of security and their interpersonal relationships throughout their lives. As an adoptive mom, my child experienced this challenge in her earliest life. After reading all the books and receiving guidance from adoption experts, I have come to realize that my relationship with her must be consistent, caring, and peaceful to the greatest extent possible. I can help her heal from those early challenges and develop the ability to securely attach to others in her future relationships.

As a special education teacher, I have found a common pattern among my students with behavioral difficulty: They sense rejection or disapproval from their parents or teachers. They have internalized the story that they are a 'bad kid' in some way, and then they take actions which align to this inaccurate label. Often, their parents don't want to send this message and they have done nothing to reinforce it. It is something their child has developed along the way. Part of my work is to persuade them that there is no such thing as a 'bad kid,' and that they are a GOOD person. I enlist the help of parents in sending this message. It takes time and repetition, but it is so worth it as the student is able to shift from self-loathing to self-determination and personal empowerment. Our children must know that we see them as good, capable people.

> Our children must know that we see them as good, capable people.

With this in mind, I encourage you to see your relationship with your child as a positive life-preserver. Even when things are strained or difficult, preserving a positive relationship is a top priority for everyone involved. This means that at all costs, we must figure out a way to get back into harmony after a difficult behavioral situation. As a parent and teacher, I have discovered some simple tools to regain peace and restore connection after a problem situation. I use these three tools daily in both of my roles: mother and teacher.

First, I try to choose restorative rather than punitive responses. Words like 'obey,' 'respect,' and 'consequence' have become almost meaningless to children. Threatening or bribing just doesn't seem to have an impact to elicit desirable behavior. An alternative perspective focuses on repairing the problem and moving forward. After a challenging behavior, I wait for your child to cool down completely and then invite them into a conversation. The key focus of the restorative conversation is, "How can we make things right again?" Then, I zip my lips and listen. Whenever things are tense in any way, I remind myself to use **lower volume**, speak more **slowly**, and say **less**. Then, I try to calmly engage the child in a peaceful chat about restoring things to the way they were before the incident. You might also find that restoring the situation works well for your child, rather than arbitrary punishment which can further fracture connection. Generate solutions together after the problem.

> Whenever things are tense in any way, I remind myself to use lower volume, speak more slowly, and say less.

Second, I help the student repair any other relationship problems which may have come about due to the situation. When a negative behavior happens, it can really upset the apple cart. Peers at school or siblings in the home may feel nervous around the student or may be irritated about the situation. This is natural. I help the student re-establish acceptance in the group by ushering them back in and emphasizing their good traits and qualities. The group most often follows suit with my example. In the home setting, this may involve healing conversations with siblings or other household members who were involved in the

TABLE 6.2 Relationship Life-Preservers with Examples

Teacher Strategies	Examples
Restorative practices: After a challenging situation, support your child in 'making things right' in order to move on in a positive way. You and your child may brainstorm ideas together. Note that forced apologies don't have much power, but perhaps your child will choose to apologize as part of the solution.	After knocking over a bookshelf in anger, your child helps you to set it back up. Your child makes a list of ideas they could use in the future if they are feeling upset at that level. Your child apologizes to the rest of the family for the intense behavior and for any property which was broken in the process.
Relationship repair: After a negative incident, the special education teacher expresses that the student is a valued member of the class and reminds them that they bring many positive aspects to the group. Engage in casual conversation about other topics of interest to restore rapport. This stage is incredibly powerful in that it conveys unconditional acceptance.	When your child is calm after a behavioral incident, you welcome them to come hang out with the family in a calm and positive way. You might choose to engage in a positive family activity which involves social interaction and evokes fun and laughter. Perhaps there is a game you all enjoy or a favorite family movie you could watch together. The idea is to relax and enjoy each other again.
Amnesia: Also called 'motivated forgetting,' individuals choose to leave the past in the past and focus on the present moment or the possibilities for the future. Let go of the negativity and, after restorative practices, move on as if it never happened. Students benefit greatly when they are offered the grace of a clean slate.	Once the negative issue is resolved, you intentionally choose to forget about the event and focus on offering your child a fresh start. If your child or another family member brings it up, encourage everyone to leave the negative event in the past and focus on the here and now, as well as a positive future. You can help everyone move on.

ACTIVITY TWENTY-SEVEN

Relationship Life-Preservers

Use this form to reflect on how you might use the relationship life-preservers to support your child after a challenging interaction or situation. It's all about returning to a peaceful, loving connection.

Restorative Practices:
Steps I can take to restore peace and harmony when needed with my child: 1. 2. 3.

Relationship Repair:
How might you convey renewed acceptance after a negative incident?   How might you help your child experience reconnection with other family members?

Amnesia:
How might 'intentional amnesia' or 'motivated forgetting' help you as a parent?   How might this practice help your child?

> I erase the incident from my mind to the greatest extent possible.

incident. Coming together again and finding a relaxed state of being with each other is very important and life-giving.

Finally, I exercise amnesia. What was that? I forgot. Oh yes. Amnesia. I erase the incident from my mind to the greatest extent possible. This can be challenging and even somewhat unnatural, but it is so important to maintain my connection with the student or with my child. I do not bring up the situation ever again, and I fully move on. If the student or my child mentions it, I change the subject quickly and focus on the good things happening in the here and now. This has been a powerful and effective practice in preserving relationships and keeping the focus on the positive. Table 6.2 provides further details and examples on relationship life-preservers. Activity 27 invites you to reflect on how these tools may support you as a parent.

Another powerful practice you can use for your child to reduce difficulty is to help them identify their day-to-day triggers and the things which build up to lead them to a behavioral challenge. Once aware of what bothers them, your child can better recognize their rising emotional responses and activate strategies to calm down. Everyone in the family can benefit from awareness of what 'sets them off' so that they can avoid these situations or take self-protective measures to prepare when triggers are unavoidable. We all have pet peeves and irritations which can add up and send us over the edge. Take the time to think about what 'gets on your nerves' and encourage your child to do the same. Then, share and discuss these so that you can come together and agree that you will try not to do these things. This can also be very powerful between siblings who tend to 'bug' each other frequently.

Perhaps this sounds like a bad idea – don't siblings try to push each other's buttons? Couldn't they use this conversation as a chance to figure out ways to drive their siblings bananas? It all depends on how you frame the conversation. If you convey that 'we're all in this together,' and 'If I know your buttons, you can know mine,' your family might become more unified and healthy through this process. Activity 28 offers a form you can

What Bothers Me?

Have each family member complete this form to identify some of the things that make you upset. Include your usual responses, whether positive or negative. Think about the words and actions of others that make you upset, as well as common situations which cause you to struggle. Then, share them with each other to avoid bothering each other.

Things that bother me . . .	My usual responses . . .

use with your child entitled 'What Bothers Me,' which invites them to share their irritations. Having each family member complete this form and then chatting about it in a lighthearted way can be a highly productive exercise. Try to have fun with this, because it can actually bring out lots of laughs!

The Q-TIP

Over and over in this book, I have highlighted the fact that many times, your child will make absolutely no sense to you at all. They are slowly accomplishing the task of finding who they are, and this means that they have to carve out a separate personality and lifestyle of their own. We hope it mirrors our values, hopes, and dreams as parents, but often, it is quite different from what we hoped for. This is okay! We must let our children be who they are and accept them along the way. At times, we can become overly distraught when our child engages in undesirable behavior or when we feel they are not responding to our guidance in life. Overreacting is never helpful, and instead, we must develop a mindset of stalwart support as our children grow up through the lovely process of trial and error we call life.

The ability to endure challenges with students without internalizing them as a personal affront can be challenging for any parent. However, developing the ability to engage in problem-solving without taking things personally is critical to your long-term happiness. The 'Q-TIP' acronym offers a helpful acronym to preserve your health and wholeness as a parent. This stands for 'Quit. Taking. It. Personally.' We indeed need to Quit-Taking-It-Personally when we struggle with understanding the actions of our child. We do what we can as parents and then we must let go and allow our children to live their lives. Their mistakes and challenges at school are not an extension of your success or failure as a parent. No one is judging you, so stop judging yourself and personalizing your child's behavior. You

> We do what we can as parents and then we must let go and allow our children to live their lives. Their mistakes and challenges at school are not an extension of your success or failure as a parent.

will maintain your happiness as a parent much more easily when you realize that the negative behavior is not about you, but rather, there are countless intervening factors involved. Table 6.3 offers examples of the Q-TIP strategy in real life. Activity 29 provides an activity entitled 'Reflections on the Q-TIP Strategy' which invites you to consider how this approach may assist you in sustaining your love for your child and ultimately your sanity.

TABLE 6.3 Examples of the 'Q-TIP' Mindset

Situation Involving Difficulty in Special Education	Unproductive Response from Special Education Teacher (Stress-Producing)	Productive Response Using the 'Q-TIP' Mindset (Stress-Busting)
Your child is overtired and refusing to come along on a family outing.	View this as active disrespect. Insist that your child come along and ignore their complaints about being tired.	Investigate why your child is so sleepy and make a better bedtime plan. Offer a 20 minute rest before leaving for the outing.
Your child expresses loud complaints when you have to say 'no' to a request. Your child tries to keep pushing until you say yes.	Give your child consequences such as a time out in their room for 'talking back' and 'disrespect.' Take away all desired items for the day so your child gets the message.	Simply state your response. Pause and state it again. Do not engage in a conversation about the situation and go find something else to do so the argument can't ensue.
Your child has promised you he will stop getting into verbal altercations in the lunchroom at school. He gets into another argument the next day during lunch.	Become downtrodden and defeated. Assume that your efforts with your child have been in vain, and they will never figure out how to make it at school. Ignore calls from his case manager to problem-solve. You are done.	Realize that your child doesn't have the skills to meet the social demands of the lunchroom setting. Explore his needs with the help of the case manager. Come together to make an alternative plan for lunchtime.
Your child becomes frustrated when directed to clean his room and says, "I hate you and I always will!"	Feel upset and sad that your child hates you and rack your brain for ways to win her over again, dwelling on this all evening.	Realize that your child doesn't hate YOU, they hate cleaning their room. Don't take it personally and hold them in your direction by simply restating it with no other reaction.

Reflections on the Q-TIP Strategy

As a parent, it can be challenging to de-personalize negative behavior from your child. However, we must realize that children are on their own journey of development and sometimes their actions will not make sense. It's not about us, and often, the best we can do is let go and love them. Complete the reflection below to consider how you might use the Q-TIP Strategy: '**Quit Taking It Personally**' when struggling with a challenging interaction or phase with your child.

What are some behaviors which 'get under your skin' or cause you to take personal offense? Why do you think these bother you so much?
What are some words of positive self-talk you can utilize 'in the moment' if you find yourself taking your child's negative behavior personally?
When you find yourself 'stuck' on a particular negative interaction with your child, how might you shift your mindset back to a positive outlook?
How might the Q-TIP Strategy help you sustain your own heart as a parent as you raise your child?

Kind, Not Permissive

We have established the importance of maintaining a positive relationship with our children. One mistake that I have seen many parents make (and which I have made myself) is to become overly permissive. In the name of relationship building, I became more of a friend than a parent. The result was a child who walked all over me, spent all of my spare cash on silly things, and lost respect for me in general. Not ideal. Being a kind, relational parent does not mean you have to say yes to everything your child wants, or spend your last dime on their every whim, or cater to their every little desire. We can easily 'create a monster,' and then we must live with our creation. With my own child, the road back from permissiveness was tricky, but I re-established boundaries and accountability while conveying that this is an act of love.

> Holding them accountable shows them that we care enough to stick to what we say and to help them learn tools for success.

Over my years in education, I have learned that setting boundaries and helping students follow them helps relationships. They don't want a permissive teacher, even if they think they do. Helping them understand how to function in the school setting is part of our job. The same rings true for you as a parent. Your child wants the safety net of your boundaries and yes even your rules. As parents, we can guide them toward their own sense of right and wrong through our relationships as we bring out the best in them. Being a loving parent doesn't mean we let go of expectations in our home, and it doesn't mean we ignore unacceptable behavior. In fact, when we become pushovers, we communicate that we don't keep our word and that we don't actually care about our children all that much. Holding them accountable shows them that we care enough to stick to what we say and to help them learn tools for success.

Today, I have learned that being an effective parent is all about balance. On one side of the scale is my warmth, kindness, caring, and genuine love for my child. On the other side is my expectation that they do what is right, follow the basic guidelines expected of them in life, and operate as a decent human being. I show my children that I trust them to have a sense of 'right and wrong' inside of themselves, and I believe in them to choose the high road. We talk about this openly in my home, and I recognize that what is 'right and wrong' will be different depending on their age and challenges. Through caring and kindness, we connect and then I can guide them toward growth in their ability to manage the expectations they are facing. Never, ever do I 'give in' or become overly permissive, but everything is enforced with one message in mind: 'We are in this together and I care about your success.' Table 6.4 offers examples of the difference between a kind yet permissive response and a kind and consistent response to various situations you may face with your child.

Expectations for your child vary across settings, and this can be confusing for them (and for all of the adults involved,

TABLE 6.4 Kind and Permissive vs. Kind and Consistent

Situation	Kind and Permissive Response	Kind and Consistent Response
Your child is constantly leaving messes around the house, including sticky dishes.	Ignore your child's habit, pick up the dishes after your child and wash them. Even though this is irritating, it isn't worth the battle to have your child pick them up.	Ask your child to bring all dirty dishes to the kitchen sink. Teach them how to soak the dishes, rinse them, or wash them depending on your child's capabilities.
Your child won't wake up for school and is consistently making the family late.	Start trying to wake your child up earlier and if this doesn't work, adjust your work schedule so you can come in a bit later in the morning.	Provide your child with an alarm clock and if they are able, teach them how to set it. Give them the time that you need to leave in the morning and expect them to be there.
Your child frequently uses profanity. It's not aggressive, but you don't like it or want it in your home.	Allow your child to use the words he wants to use so that he can be himself. If this includes profanity, that's part of who he is. Tell him to clean up his language at school so he doesn't get in trouble.	Model appropriate language as much as you can. Explain your expectations to your child and address it if you hear the undesirable language. Give a simple direction: "We don't use those words." Then, move on.

The Unwritten Rules

Helping your child understand the different expectations you need to follow at school, at home, or in another setting you go to often can help them avoid problems and reduce stress for your family as a whole. Discuss the 'unwritten rules' which exist in different settings and record them here. Use this to provide reminders as needed for your child.

Expectations at School:	
List the rules you follow for what you do and say at school which may not be the 'official' written rules in the handbook.	
Expectations at Home:	
List the rules you follow for what you do and say at home which may be different from the rules at school	
Expectations at _____:	
Choose another setting you go to often. List the rules you follow in this setting for what you do and say.	

ACTIVITY THIRTY-ONE

H.A.L.T.S. Interventions

Human beings are at our worst when we are **hungry, angry, lonely, tired, or stressed**. These conditions can cause 'bad moods' which lead to conflict and strife. Complete this form to plan for how you may identify and meet these needs to prevent undesirable behaviors by avoiding these situations.

Hungry: What are some routines and resources you can establish to avoid excessive hunger?
Angry: How might you help your child recognize and calm when angry?
Lonely: How might you connect with your child when they are lonely? Remember that they won't always tell you that they are feeling this way, so stay vigilant.
Tired: How might you utilize routines and resources to avoid excessive tiredness?
Stressed: How might you come alongside your child when they are experiencing stress?

for that matter). As parents, we can help our children tremendously when we help them identify and adhere to contextual expectations. Our children navigate many different worlds, such as school, home, and perhaps the workplace for older students, and each of these environments involves varying expectations for conduct. At school, our children probably experience vastly different expectations from class to class at the secondary level. Helping your child to recognize the 'unwritten rules' which exist across settings can support their success overall.

> Children need the opportunity to identify exactly what is expected of them between the settings they navigate and build the skills to manage these shifting requirements.

Children need the opportunity to identify exactly what is expected of them between the settings they navigate and build the skills to manage these shifting requirements. This may involve both direct instruction and modeling at school, depending on the student and the situation. At home, this means clearly identifying the implied expectations in various contexts and then helping your child build the skills to shift between settings. This is challenging and in fact, many adults still struggle with this in their lives. Activity 30 offers an activity entitled 'The Unwritten Rules' which you can complete with your child to help develop this understanding and support your child in meeting unspoken expectations. As you explore the 'unwritten rules' with child, you help convey the importance of boundaries. This balances relational interaction with structure and accountability. Children must learn that boundaries matter in order to survive and thrive as adults.

The Soda Can

Imagine a can of soda sitting on a table. You approach the can, decide to take a sip, and it blows up in your face. Little did you know, only moments before another member of your family had shaken the can vigorously and set it on the table. You didn't shake up the can, but you were the one to open it. Thus, you were the one with a big, huge mess. This can be likened to our

154 offers an activity entitled 'H.A.L.T.S.

children at times. Life may be 'shaking up the can,' and we are often the ones who get to open it as parents. There are so many factors which influence student actions which are outside of our control. How do we help them? We can meet their needs in a proactive way whenever possible.

As established earlier in the chapter, behavior is communication. When your child acts out, the question is: What is this person trying to tell me? How can I meet the unmet need? You will increase the likelihood of emotional health when you realize that although you cannot 'control' your child's behavior and stop negative events entirely, you can identify elements of the environment which may incite undesirable behavior. At times, your child will not be at their best due to temporary conditions in their lives. The H.A.L.T.S. acronym stands for: Hungry, Angry, Lonely, Tired, and Stressed (Turner, 2018). Human beings in any of these states may be more likely to demonstrate undesirable behaviors because they have immediate unmet needs. Activity 31 offers an activity entitled 'H.A.L.T.S. Interventions' which you can complete to support your child through these difficulties. It is of note that you as a parent may also use the H.A.L.T.S. acronym to reflect on your own feelings and meet your own needs in order to be at your best.

Conclusion

No matter how wonderful and amazing your child is, there will be times when their behavior demands intervention. Depending on our approach, this process can be a source of frustration or it can be productive and helpful for your child. Realize that your child is always communicating with you, whether they are speaking or not. Their behavior is loaded with underlying messages about what they need, want, and hope for. Try to pay attention to their unspoken words and be proactive to solve problems before they start. When things do go wrong, strive to return to a healthy connection with your child as soon as possible. Opt to try to restore the situation to peace and make things right, rather than focusing on punishment. Convey your full acceptance of your child and help them repair any issues with other family members. Once all is well, practice amnesia and try to erase the negative incident from your mind. Your child needs a fresh start and a new chance.

Remember that you can be a kind, caring, genuine, loving parent without being permissive. In fact, your child wants the safety of accountability, and boundaries show that you care about them. Even when difficulties occur and emotions run high, strive to de-escalate situations as much as you can. Remember to Q-TIP, or Quit Taking It Personally, as much as you can, realizing that your child's behavior is most often not about you. Other factors shook up the soda can, and you were the lucky one who opened it to take a sip. Invite your child to share what bothers them and try to minimize their triggers. Also, keep your eye out for H.A.L.T.S., when your child is hungry, angry, lonely, tired or stressed, and intervene early to meet their needs.

Chapter 6 Simple Snapshot

- ◆ Remember that behavior includes hidden messages to help you understand your child.
- ◆ Take steps to preserve family relationships to preserve your own peace.
- ◆ Identify what bothers your students and then take steps to prevent their triggers.
- ◆ Don't take it personally when your child struggles – it's usually not really about you.
- ◆ Being kind and loving doesn't mean you don't enforce boundaries.
- ◆ Help your child understand the 'unwritten rules' for various contexts they must navigate.
- ◆ Be proactive by watching out for H.A.L.T.S.: Hungry, Angry, Lonely, Tired, and Stressed.

Chapter 6 Reflection Questions

Use the following questions to reflect on what you have learned in the chapter. You may choose to journal about them or discuss them with a partner or small group to gain further insights.

1. What are some of the behavioral difficulties you have experienced in your family? What has worked and what hasn't?
2. How might you use the ideas in this chapter to restore peace and connection after an undesirable behavior incident?
3. What are your thoughts on the premise that behavior is communication? How do you connect with the soda can analogy?
4. How might the Q-TIP (Quit Taking It Personally) apply to your life as a parent? What are some steps you might take if you find yourself personalizing your child's behavior?
5. How might you help your child understand the unwritten rules in different contexts? Where does your child struggle most and how might they be unclear on the expectations in this setting?
6. How might the acronym H.A.L.T.S. (Hungry, Angry, Lonely, Tired, and Stressed) help you support your child? Which of these presents the biggest challenge for them?

References

Chazin, K.T. & Ledford, J.R. (2016). Challenging behavior as communication. In *Evidence-based instructional practices for young children with autism and other disabilities.* Retrieved from http://ebip.vkcsites.org/challenging-behavior-as-communication.

Galvin, G. (2016). *Survey: Students face challenges outside the classroom.* U.S. News and World Report. https://www.usnews.com/news/national-news/articles/2016-11-21/scholastic-survey-more-must-be-done-to-help-students-outside-the-classroom.

Greene, R. (2015). Collaborative and proactive solutions. *Therapeutic Parenting Journal*, no. 5. https://www.attachmenttraumanetwork.org/wp-content/uploads/Collaborative-Problem-Solving-Dec-2015.pdf.

Schröder, M., Lüdtke, J., Fux, E., Izat, Y., Bolten, M., Gloger-Tippelt, G., Suess, G.J., & Schmid, M. (2019). Attachment disorder and attachment theory – Two sides of one medal or two different coins? *Comprehensive Psychiatry*, vol. 95, pp. 152139–152139. doi:10.1016/j.comppsych.2019.152139.

Scott, T.M. (2017). Training classroom management with preservice special education teachers: Special education challenges in a general education world. *Teacher Education and Special Education*, vol. 40, no. 2, pp. 97–101. doi:10.1177/0888406417699051.

Turner, C. (2018). *How are you feeling? Take a minute to HALT for your health*. Goodtherapy.org. https://www.goodtherapy.org/blog/how-are-you-feeling-take-minute-halt-for-your-health-0515184.

7

We're in This Together

Kristina Hernandez loved her daughter Angelica with every molecule of her heart. She had raised her on her own with a fierce kind of love which shielded Angelica from the many dangers and vulnerabilities the world may present to her. Early in her preschool years, Angelica was identified as an individual with autism spectrum disorder and had been receiving services in early childhood special education settings since this time. Now, it was time for a transition which concerned Kristina very deeply: the transition to kindergarten.

When Sharon Robinson graduated from college with a degree in special education, she promised herself one thing: she would love her students. Ms Robinson had struggled in school and received services in special education to support her academic gaps and emotional needs. Her family had moved 16 times between kindergarten and her senior year due to issues with her father's work and struggles to keep up with ever-increasing rental fees for their meager apartments. Sharon never felt at home in the school setting and thus, she had decided to commit herself to creating belonging and sharing love every day.

As a kindergarten teacher, Ms. Robinson conveyed warmth, kindness and most importantly, unconditional acceptance. No matter who walked through the door of her classroom, she committed to love them and accept them as they are. Posted on her wall, she displayed the words:

"I See You… I Like You… I'm Glad You're Here… Love, Ms. Robinson."

The evening of the kindergarten open house, Ms. Robinson stood at her door awaiting families. Parents had been invited to come in with their child to explore the classroom space and start getting to know the environment. The first parent to arrive looked timid and concerned. Her daughter seemed equally bashful and didn't say a word.

"Hi, I'm Kristina, and this is my daughter Angelica, and I'm really nervous."

Ms. Robinson offered her hand and the two exchanged a charged moment heavy with a parent's hopes, dreams and fears, and a teacher's warmth, kindness and welcoming spirit.

"Tell me more about why you are nervous?" Ms. Robinson asked.

"Well Angelica has autism and transitions can be really tough. She was finally settled in at preschool and now it's time for another change."

DOI: 10.4324/9781003364443-10

"That makes sense. All I know is I can't wait to have fun with Angelica in kindergarten!" Ms. Robinson knelt and whispered warmly, "I think you're going to love it here!"

Angelica giggled and stepped out from behind her mother, just a bit.

As they conversed, Ms. Hernandez's fears and concerns melted away in the face of Ms. Robinson's open, genuine, caring presence. Ms. Robinson conveyed that she loved being a teacher and that she would fully accept Angelica as a fully included member of the classroom. Kristina Hernandez was ready to entrust her precious child to Ms. Robinson's care during the school day, which was a huge relief. By the end of the conversation, Angelica was laughing along with her mom and teacher, and offered an enthusiastic high five at the end of the conversation!

Oh that every teacher could be like Sharon Robinson. If only every educator decided to send the message 'I see you, I like you, and I'm glad you're here.' As a special educator for nearly 20 years, I have found that when students receive this message, they bask in the glow of true acceptance and they thrive. This means that I get to become a purveyor of hope, and this can be powerful for my students. Empathy and unconditional acceptance are two of the most powerful practices we can choose to implement as human beings sharing in this human experience. The impact of these approaches can make a world of positive difference for our children.

In truth, not all educators have the philosophy or skills to support your child in experiencing belonging. I wish I could tell you differently, but I also need to be honest. As parents, this means that we can help our children thrive by helping them enjoy full acceptance and the safety of belonging in our family environments. At times, the stress of parenting and the impact of a family member's disability can cause strife and challenges in relationships. I believe that the more we can come together in unity, the more our children will thrive. Just like Ms. Robinson, we can send the message 'I see who you are… I like who you are… and I'm so glad to be your parent.' This message can help your child so much, even on the difficult days.

This chapter is focused on how your child and your family can benefit from the premise that **'We're in this together.'** No member of our family faces their problems alone and without loving support at their back. No matter how challenging things get, family unity can help your child thrive. In my experience, children best thrive when they have a sense of safety, and true belonging is a source of this security. As we celebrate our children for who they are, we may see greater growth and positive change. Unconditional love may come easily to you as a parent, but unconditional acceptance of your child's needs, quirks, and idiosyncrasies can be more challenging. This chapter will help us explore the power of unconditional acceptance, as well as practical strategies to implement this philosophy in real life. The more a child experiences deep acceptance, the better we keep their hope alive. "A key component of this is to cultivate and express positive emotions like joy, love, gratitude, and awe" (Hammond, 2017). When we fully accept and celebrate our children, we enjoy them more, convey authentic love, express gratitude for them, and even find ourselves in awe at their abilities and resilience.

> Unconditional love may come easily to you as a parent, but unconditional acceptance of your child's needs, quirks, and idiosyncrasies can be more challenging.

This chapter will also invite you to review the beautiful story of your family in order to come together. You will also be invited to define your family's shared interests and preferences. Empathy, or the ability to consider another's full perspective, can help further deepen connection and unity within your family. The chapter

Key Themes

- ◆ The choice to practice unconditional acceptance every day can benefit both you and your child.
- ◆ Every individual in the family has a personal history and your family also has a shared story which can help you come together.
- ◆ Culture includes elements such as foods, traditions, art, and preferred activities. Defining the culture of your family can be a fun and unifying experience.
- ◆ Empathy is the ability to fully take on another person's perspective including how they feel in various situations. Empathy is a powerful tool for connection with your child.
- ◆ Coming together with a focus on shared goals, hopes, and dreams can be hope-giving and motivating for all family members.

will invite you into a new way of thinking about empathy which is more than simply 'walking in someone else's shoes.' Finally, you will explore tools and ideas to bring families together based on shared hopes and dreams. After reading the material in this chapter and completing the activities, the hope is that you will enjoy a greater sense of connection to help all family members grow.

In the Same Boat

Every year, I spend at least one week entirely immersed in nature. On the border between the United States and Canada, there lies a hidden gem known well to my fellow Minnesotans but lesser known outside of my humble home. Nearly 2 million acres (4,400 square kilometers) of pristine wilderness remains virtually untouched by human influence known as the Boundary Waters Canoe Area. A limited number of passes are sold each year, and I am always first in line for my opportunity to voyage into the quietude. Once inside, you find yourself at the mercy of nature with the pack on your back and the canoe beneath you. Nothing more. No motors. No cell phone signal. No convenience. Just you, mother nature, and a paddle in your hands. The further you journey in, the more you hope you packed well. It's incredibly challenging, incredibly rewarding, and deeply restorative.

Why am I telling you about this? Well, one of the key skills necessary to enjoy such a trip is the ability to chart your course and paddle (and paddle and paddle and paddle) your canoe. Most often this happens with a partner paddling along with you. Sometimes, things are a piece of cake. The wind is at your back, you know exactly where you are going, and the sun is shining. At other times, you find yourself paddling into the wind, fighting white-capped waves, and losing track of your course. In these moments, you might find yourself frustrated with your partner. Maybe they aren't paddling hard enough. Maybe they misread the map and you don't agree about which way you should go. This is normal in any

> Unless you can come together, coordinate your efforts, and agree on a path, you will find yourself lost and exhausted.

human relationship, but here's the thing: Unless you can come together, coordinate your efforts, and agree on a path, you will find yourself lost and exhausted.

This analogy has direct applications to family life. Like it or not, raising our children means that we are in the same canoe. When our children are young, we take on the role of reading the map, navigating, and steering the canoe. Our little ones get to enjoy the ride as they mindlessly paddle along. However, as they grow older and develop in their identity, they need to take on the leadership role for their lives more and more. We must hand them the map and trust that they can figure it out. For a while, this transition can create difficulty. You may feel as if you are paddling in different directions causing the canoe to come to a standstill. The secret? Trust your child. Let go. Realize that you have prepared them to succeed and you can support them by paddling along in the same direction. If you get lost, you will be okay. Help them regain their path if they need it or offer them time and space to figure it out for themselves. Most importantly, don't work against them. After all, you are all in the same boat!

> Trust your child. Let go. Realize that you have prepared them to succeed and you can support them by paddling along in the same direction.

Unconditional Acceptance

Let me begin with a bit of honesty – you will not feel absolutely thrilled and excited to be a parent every day… and your child will not always feel thrilled to interact with you as their parent. This is completely and totally okay. It's natural. It's normal. It's called life. When you find yourself butting heads with your child or struggling to connect, this is a chance to explore creative ways to open your heart a little bit more to find a place of love and acceptance. Ask yourself the right questions, like, 'why is this difficult for me?' and 'what is actually bothering me about this situation?' Humans learn and grow from each other, and we can use those difficult relationships as a chance at introspection.

If every moment with our children was always sunshine, rainbows, and butterflies, we may not appreciate the goodness quite as much. Embrace the struggle and know that once you overcome an obstacle together, you will deepen the life-giving connection you share with your child. Remember the tools offered in Chapter 6 such as depersonalizing or the premise that the struggle isn't about you. Your child is not trying to challenge you or make your life difficult. They are growing up and defining themselves.

> Humans learn and grow from each other, and we can use those difficult relationships as a chance at introspection.

I suggest you commit to the premise of 'unconditional acceptance' of your child just as they are. This means that no matter what, you will accept your child for the person they are becoming, even if they don't completely align to your ideas, goals, and desires. This doesn't mean you accept undesirable behavior, but you accept your child as a valuable individual who is a part of a learning journey. In order to help you fully accept your child, it may help to remember a few simple truths which I have learned from thousands of conversations with parents over the years. These include:

- ◆ **Your child is not an extension of you.** Too often, parents perceive that their child is a reflection of their skills, abilities, or knowledge of how to raise children. Nope. Not in the least. When your child struggles, this is not your fault. Try to refrain from judging yourself or fearing the judgment of others. Celebrate and refocus on the successes (but remember, your child's successes are also their own – with your loving support).
- ◆ **Your child is not your project.** There is no such thing as the perfect parent or the perfect child. Raising children is not an assignment on which you can earn an A+. There is no such thing as 'achievement' as a parent, and instead, it is a journey of love, grace, and flexibility. So, relax and realize that parenting doesn't need to be hard work to make sure your children 'turn out okay.' Rather, it is something to savor and enjoy as much as possible.

♦ **Your child is not your enemy.** This one can be so tough. With my own teenagers, I have gone through periods of months in which they felt the need to argue with every word I spoke. It happens. When the complications of a disability come into play, the oppositional relationship can be even more prominent and exhausting. Remember that even though it can feel like a battle at times, you are both on the same side: your child's success.

♦ **Your child is not your peer.** Enmeshment occurs when children aren't given the space and boundaries to learn independent skills such as emotional regulation (Kivisto et al., 2015). Although we approach our children with love, we must realize that we are their parent and not their peer. Oversharing about our own emotional struggles, overhelping when they face challenges, and neglecting to enforce boundaries can all lead to serious difficulties for everyone in the family.

The truth is, your child is a unique individual who is trying to figure out a life which works for them. As a parent, you are their number one fan, their source of support when they need it, and an ally in supporting them in solving their problems. You are also a guide and a source of accountability as your child learns boundaries. You fulfill these roles much more easily when you commit to accepting your child for who they are and use this as the starting point for all of your interactions with them. In this way, you communicate that they are good, that they are valuable, and that you love them for who they are. Oh that every child could have that foundation! Simply knowing that someone is in your corner no matter what can have an incredible impact.

In practicing unconditional acceptance, love and grace are the names of the game. This doesn't mean we let everyone run wild, willy nilly, into complete chaos. We can set the stage for improvement in any relationship by maintaining love, assuming that our children are doing the best they can with what they have and upholding our expectations. You will find a way to be kind, yet firm. When I think back over my teaching career, the students who stand out the most are those who gave me a run

Unconditional Acceptance Reflection

Use this form to reflect on how you might practice unconditional acceptance with your child, especially when you are experiencing struggles in your relationship.

Practicing Unconditional Acceptance:	
Three things I can easily accept about my child: 1. 2. 3.	Three things I struggle to accept about my child: 1. 2. 3.
Potential benefits of unconditional acceptance:	
Three benefits I enjoy when I choose unconditional acceptance: 1. 2. 3.	Three ways unconditional acceptance can benefit my child and my family. 1. 2. 3.
Strategies to practice unconditional acceptance:	
Three strategies I may use to remind myself to practice unconditional acceptance include: 1. 2. 3.	

for my money at first! They pushed every button they could find and put me to the test to see how I would respond. Once they discovered that I would remain steady, strong, caring, and kind, they moved into a place of trust and the relationships flourished. For many of them, their entire school experience improved.

In the same way, you can cultivate unconditional acceptance as a parent. Imagine that the next time you are in a difficult situation with your child, you choose to look past the struggle and see the human being in front of you. Perhaps you are already good at this. You easily approach your parenting from a place of love and grace. This is absolutely awesome, and I look up to you. For me, it takes intentional effort to choose my actions and words carefully so that I send my children the message that I am on their side. When your child perceives that adults are constantly trying to 'fix' them, they may internalize the message that they are broken. When your child perceives that they belong just as they are, they can grow and thrive from a grounded place of safety and security. Activity 32 offers an activity entitled 'Unconditional Acceptance Reflection' to help you put this powerful approach into practice.

> When your child perceives that they belong just as they are, they can grow and thrive from a grounded place of safety and security.

Sharing Personal Histories

As we grow up as human beings, we develop a unique personal history, which shapes who we are and how we see the world. This is true for every single individual on this spinning blue planet. Culture has been defined as the features of every existence shared by people in a place or time (Merriam-Webster, 2022). Cultural influence begins with our earliest interactions as human beings and creates the lens through which we see the world. Your family has a culture of its own, whether you are aware of it or not, which includes elements such as foods, traditions, daily habits, and preferred activities. Why does this matter? Well, defining and enjoying your shared family culture can be a unifying experience. This can also help your child develop pride and security in who they are.

You might start by sharing your family's story. How did you come to the life you are living today? What history do you know and what lessons might be learned from those who came before you. In many families, such as mine, there were painful events and challenges which seemed almost insurmountable. The more our children learn about the strength of those in the past, the more they might pick up the torch and run with it into the future. It helps for them to know that life isn't easy and that struggle is part of the deal. However, we don't set up our tent and camp out in the struggle. We carry on, and somehow things get better as the journey continues.

We also serve our children well when we invite them to share their own stories. When we provide avenues for them to share the way they see the world and the stories which have shaped who they are, we tell our children that we value them and that they matter to us. The important note here is that we don't speak FOR them. Instead, we ask them questions and invite them to share what stands out as important over the stories of their lives. I am always surprised when I ask my children about their fondest memories because the things they remember are often vastly different from what I might expect. These are beautiful conversations which can help deepen connection.

> When we provide avenues for them to share the way they see the world and the stories which have shaped who they are, we tell our children that we value them and that they matter to us.

When we see our children as unique individuals with rich stories to share, they learn that their importance and potential are not defined by a label on an individual education plan, a set of test scores in a computerized database, or a list of letter grades on a transcript. School practices such as these have constantly put our children into little boxes, and as parents, we can help them break free into who they really are. They are human participants in their own lives poised to accomplish great things and realize their full potential with the support of a team who truly cares about them.

Sure, the school may have a file of information on our child in the world of special education, but they must know that they are so much more than the information we read in these documents. Too often, the file will tell the story of the deficits rather than the strengths. It will leave out the rich and meaningful memories which have shaped who our children are. As a teacher, I usually read the file with the expectation that it won't give me the full story. I get to discover the magic in each student as I build a relationship with them in real live practice. The negative information in a pile of paperwork will not bias me to expect anything but the best from my students!

You might follow a series of simple steps to identify the moments which matter most to your child in their young life. This process may also involve solidifying the culture in your family to come together in a more meaningful way. Finally, you might choose to share this information with school personnel to further deepen their understanding of your amazing child. The process may look something like this:

1. Invite each member of the family to complete 'Activity 33,' 'My Life Map,' which offers a structured activity your child may use to share key memories or moments which stand out to them in their lives. You can view an example to help you envision what this may look like. Your child may choose to use drawings and words or cut images from magazines depending on their ability level and needs.

2. As a family, come together to complete 'Activity 34' entitled 'Our Family Culture.' This invites you to list the key people, places, and things which make your family unique and which bring you together. You can then create statements to unify you further as a celebration of your shared identity.

3. Share these tools with the school if you wish. Your child's team may especially enjoy viewing their life map in order

to better understand what has shaped them as a person. This may be particularly impactful if the information on the life map relates to your child's engagement in the school setting. The better school personnel know your child's personal history, the better they can craft learning experiences aligned to their unique perspectives (Figure 7.1) (Jorgensen, 2021).

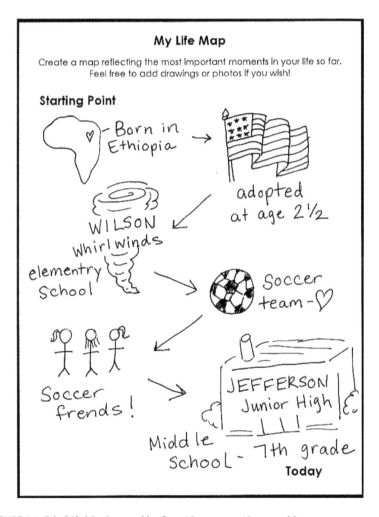

FIGURE 7.1 'My Life Map' created by Samri Jorgensen, 12 years old.

My Life Map

Create a map reflecting the most important moments in your
life so far. Feel free to add drawings or photos.

Starting Point

Today

Our Family Culture

Family Members	Favorite Memories	Favorite Foods
Favorite Places	Sayings in Our Family	Favorite Songs or Stories

Things which are important to us:

In the space below, complete each sentence to celebrate the culture in your family:

In this family, we

_____

In this family, we

_____

In this family, we

_____

In this family, we

_____

In this family, we

_____

In this family, we

_____

The Empathy Check

One of the easiest things we can do for our children is to pay attention. Why? Because no other tool may be more powerful than empathy in the lives of our children. Empathy is so much more than simply 'walking in someone else's shoes.' Rather, it has been defined as the ability to sense others' feelings and how they see things, take an active interest in their concerns, and listen to them attentively to understand their point of view (Taylor, 2018). Showing our children empathy may be directly likened to showing them love. When we fully accept them for who they are, the next step is to try to understand the way they see the world and their life situations.

> Showing our children empathy may be directly likened to showing them love.

The importance of empathy is woven throughout this book, just as empathy can be woven throughout our parenting practices. The more we can go beyond just putting ourselves in our child's shoes, seeing the world out of their eyes, sharing in emotions and 'feeling' right along with them, the more we come alongside them in the allyship which can lead to their lasting success. This approach is at the heart of unconditional acceptance as we strive to fully understand and embrace our children for all that they are.

What does practicing empathy look like in the real life of a parent? Activity 35 provides a reflection entitled 'The Empathy Check,' which invites you to think about various areas of your home and how they may impact your child's life experience. The goal is to create spaces and situations that allow your child to relax, restore, and enjoy life as much as possible. When our children are set up for success, we can relax and enjoy a less stressful experience as parents. You may choose to utilize the empathy check to discuss other environments with your child, such as family gatherings, restaurants, and of course, school. The hope is to better understand their challenges to help them manage the demands of varying environments.

ACTIVITY THIRTY-FIVE

The Empathy Check

Part of understanding your child and supporting their success is trying to see the world and their life experiences through their eyes. Complete the chart below to reflect on your child's perspective.

Area of Life	Reflection Question
HOUSEHOLD STIMULI: This includes the sensory experience of living in your home. Sensory input includes what your home sounds like, looks like, feels like, etc. This also includes the physical layout of your living space and how this may feel for your child.	How might your child experience the sounds, smells, tastes, tactile and visual stimuli in your home?
FAMILY RELATIONSHIPS: Describes the interpersonal dynamics of the members of your home. This includes the nature of communication, sharing resources and connections among the individuals who make up your family.	How might your child be experiencing relationships within your family?
IMPLIED MESSAGES: This includes the unspoken messages your child may be receiving, both positive and negative, from the experience of being a member of your family. This might also include the unspoken messages they are trying to send to you.	What implied messages might your child be sending or receiving?

Look To a Bright Future

This chapter is all about coming together as a family unit. Activities such as 'My Life Map' and 'Our Family Culture' can help you take a look back and see where your family has come from and how you have grown through individual and shared experiences. Activities such as 'The Empathy Check' can help you take a close look at what is happening right now for your child and develop a plan for meeting current needs. The final area in which your family may find unity and strength is in looking ahead to your child's bright future. Yes. I said BRIGHT future. The more you believe that your child will succeed and find an adult life of happiness and as much independence as possible, the more likely it is that this will come true!

Children are born with an unanswered question: "Who am I and what is my place in the world?" and they spend their lives trying to answer this question (Brummelman and Thomaes, 2017). As parents, we share in this question and it can sometimes be absolutely terrifying. What will life look like for my child in the future? Will they find a way to be self-sufficient? Will they find fulfillment? Happiness? Love? The honest answer is this: There is absolutely no way to know. None of us have a crystal ball which works with 100% accuracy, and even the best fortune teller can't give you the comforting details you might desire with complete certainty. What I do know is that the more we can believe in a positive outcome, the more likely it is that it might happen. As mentioned in Chapter 4, a self-fulfilling prophecy is a phenomenon in which what we believe tends to come true (Lopez, 2017). Come together based on the belief that the future will be BETTER than expected, and you just might find this coming true!

> Come together based on the belief that the future will be BETTER than expected, and you just might find this coming true!

Activity 36 invites you to create a vision with your child regarding future dreams and goals. This may be a useful tool at any age, but it takes on particular importance as your child

Shared Hopes and Dreams

Use this form to think about lifelong goals for your child. Review this together and create hopes and dreams together as a family.

	Where are we now?	Where do we hope to be in 5 years?
Education		
Work/ Career		

Things about the future we feel good about:

Things about the future we are concerned about:

Our hopes and dreams:

nears the transition from school to work. Notice that this tool is designed to be completed together and in truth, it is meant to be a discussion-starter. Your conversations can be a source of hope as you consistently help your child return to the belief that the future is full of wonderful possibilities, and that it is not a thing to be feared. No one likes uncertainty. We all want guarantees that everything will come up roses. This just isn't real life. Instead, we can choose hope and optimism over despair and cynicism over and over (and over and over and over).

Conclusion

For better or worse, you and your child are in the same boat. You will all enjoy the journey much more if you learn to coordinate your efforts and paddle along together. You can offer a firm foundation for your child and support their success when you make the choice to practice unconditional acceptance of exactly who they are. Often, our children have quirks and idiosyncrasies which can become a bit tiresome. We spend more time with them than anyone, and it is completely natural that at times, we may find ourselves a bit worn down by their words or actions. We can choose to accept the person that they are and convey our love while we guide them toward greater social understanding and positive interaction. Our children need the persistent message 'I see who you are, I like who you are, and I'm so glad to be your parent.'

We can also empower our children by inviting them to share what is important to them in their lives. Inviting them to share their fondest memories and key moments can help you connect more deeply. Empathy is more than seeing a different perspective. It is trying to experience life through the eyes, ears, and feelings of another. Considering how your child is experiencing life can help you meet their needs. Finally, it is important to look ahead with confidence that although we don't know what life holds for us, it will be something great. The more we expect great things for our child, the more likely it is that these dreams will come true.

Chapter 7 Simple Snapshot

- ◆ Unconditional acceptance means embracing your child exactly as they are.
- ◆ Learning about your child's personal history in terms of what is important to them can help deepen your connection.
- ◆ Every family has a unique culture. Identify the people, places, routines, traditions, and values which are shared within your family to help cultivate unity.
- ◆ The 'empathy check' involves taking a moment to consider how your child might experience various contexts to help them manage this effectively.
- ◆ Come together with a shared, hopeful vision for a bright future. Persistent optimism might just pay off!

Chapter 7 Reflection Questions

Use the following questions to reflect on what you have learned in the chapter. You may choose to journal about them or discuss them with a partner or small group to gain further insights.

1. What is your perspective on the concept of 'unconditional acceptance'? How might this approach help you as a parent? How may this be difficult?
2. Where do you find your family most unified and where do you seem to be working against each other? How might you come together and start moving in the same direction?
3. What are some key events in your child's life and how did these impact who they are?
4. What are some elements of your family's culture? How might you celebrate and enjoy these together to deepen your connection?
5. How might the 'empathy check' support you in making your child's experiences more manageable in various contexts?

6. What are some of your hopes and dreams for your child? How might you choose to believe in positive outcomes and a bright future?

References

Brummelman, E. & Thomaes, S. (2017). When parents' praise inflates, children's self-esteem deflates. *Child Development*, vol. 88, no. 6, Wiley Subscription Services, Inc, pp. 1799–809.

Hammond, Zaretta. (2017). *We all can be authentic merchants of hope.* Culturally Responsive Teaching and the Brain, https://crtandthebrain.com/we-all-can-be-authentic-merchants-of-hope/.

Jorgensen, S. (2022). *My Life Map* [line drawing]. Anoka Middle School for the Arts. Anoka, MN, USA.

Kivisto, K.L., Welsh, D.P., Darling, N., & Culpepper, C.L. (2015). Family enmeshment, adolescent emotional dysregulation, and the moderating role of gender. *Journal of Family Psychology*, vol. *29*, no. 4, pp. 604–613, doi:10.1037/fam0000118.

Lopez, F. (2017). Altering the trajectory of the self-fulfilling prophecy: Asset-based pedagogy and classroom dynamics. *Journal of Teacher Education*, vol. 68, no. 2, pp. 193–212, doi:10.1177/0022487116685751.

Merriam-Webster. (2022). Culture. In *Merriam-Webster.com*. Retrieved September 19, 2022, from https://www.merriam-webster.com/dictionary/culture.

Taylor, M. (2018). Building a culture of empathy in the classroom. *Teachers Matter*, vol. 39, pp. 32–35.

Connecting with Yourself

The final section of this book is all about YOU. Yes. YOU. Perhaps you cringe when you read this. Maybe it sounds selfish or indulgent. Maybe your own life, needs, and perspectives have fallen by the wayside as your parenting tasks have eclipsed all else. Too often, parents of children with special needs neglect their own well-being and personal needs for the sake of their children. The final section of this book will offer go-to strategies you can use to take better care of yourself and exercise persistent self-kindness. The concept of self-care has become a buzzword in public discourse. Often, people think of self-care as candlelit baths or pedicures. While these might be delightful, they may not have a lasting impact on your overall well-being. We will explore tools to help you truly manage the depth of challenges you face as a parent to better connect with yourself. Rather than offering temporary solutions, this section provides evidence-based approaches to nourish yourself more fully, manage the demands of daily life with calm and ease, and commit to a life of gratitude, acceptance, and purpose. Tending to your own health and wholeness will support your ability to parent your child from a place of consistency and authentic love. This section will help you find solid ground on which to walk the path of parenting with confidence and greater ease.

DOI: 10.4324/9781003364443-11

8

Beyond Self-Care to Self-Nourishment

Jamie Scalia's son Max was in kindergarten. He was loving every minute of it and succeeding at a level beyond everyone's expectations. Max had cerebral palsy and struggled at times with his processing speed and his motor skills. His teacher Ms. Henning was a huge cheerleader for Max and was doing a beautiful job adapting lessons and materials to meet his needs. She still found ways to challenge him and Max felt included right along with his peers. Jamie was thrilled to see her son thriving!

Jamie had to admit, there was a bit of a learning curve to being a kindergarten parent. She was new to everything in that Max was an only child, and at times, she felt a little lost. The school year began with a flurry of forms and paperwork, not to mention the fact that she would soon be attending Max's first Individual Education Planning meeting at the elementary level. Jamie tried her best to stay up to date on everything, but it seemed that Max's 'take home folder' was constantly overflowing with new information, as well as numerous emails from the school and from Ms. Henning. Along with her high-demand job and her life as a single parent, it all could get to be a bit much at times.

One afternoon, Jamie was going through Max's folder and noticed a flier about an upcoming 'Fall Party.' The invitation described the celebration and asked for parent volunteers. Parents could also sign up to donate various products for the party. Finally, the invitation stated that each child would have a 'take-home' project which they would share during the party.

'This sounds like so much fun! I'm going to sign up,' Jamie thought. She crafted a quick email requesting the afternoon off of work and then filled out the form to indicate that she would be happy to volunteer. She also agreed to bring in paper cups and napkins. With a smile, she replaced the completed form in Max's folder to send it back to Ms. Henning. She left a reminder in her online calendar to pick up cups and napkins. 'All set.' She thought. A few days later, Max brought home his 'take home' project which was to decorate the outline of a pumpkin. She set him up at the kitchen table with a set of markers and told

DOI: 10.4324/9781003364443-12

him to do his best to color the pumpkin. She also told him he could draw some leaves or stems if he would like. In her mind, this was his project and he should create what he wanted to share.

As the day of the fall party approached, things seemed to surmount at work. A new project had fallen on her desk and Jamie was taking on some new responsibilities. She was excited for the opportunity, but feeling a little swamped. When party day arrived, she ended up starting the day at the office, tying up some loose ends and then flying to the store for the paper cups and napkins. She hit an unexpected mid-day traffic jam on the way to Max's school and ended up making it to the party 15 minutes late. 'Better late than never,' she thought.

The festivities were a blast. The children played counting and math games with cute little pumpkin counting cubes, engaged in a round of fall bingo and made rubbings with fall leaves. They shared in some tasty snacks and it was so much fun to meet the five other parents who had volunteered. As the kindergarteners danced along with a fun fall Youtube video, Ms. Henning called the volunteers together for a huddle.

"The last part of the party is a chance for each child to share their take-home project. I'm going to have them go to their cubbies to take them out, and then we'll go around in a circle for them to share. Please help monitor the hallway as they grab their projects, and then they can join me on the rug for circle sharing. Thanks!" As the parents moved to complete the task, Jamie's stomach dropped to her feet. She knew she was forgetting something and now she realized what it was: Max's take-home project. Truth be told, she hadn't seen it since that first afternoon when Max started to work on it.

As the children gathered for circle time, Jamie's despair deepened. Every single child not only remembered their take-home project, they were absolutely beautiful. It looked as if their parents had bought out the craft store designing elaborate pumpkins with special stickers, glitter, and beautiful designs. Glancing at Max, Jamie noticed something in his hands. There he sat with his crumpled, very much unimpressive project. His pumpkin had some orange shading on it, and Max had tried his very best to draw a stem and leaf. Compared to the other projects, Max's looked like…. well… it was made by a kindergartner.

The group took turns sharing about their projects and it quickly became evident that most of them had relied on their parents to come up with their creations. Ms. Henning smiled and nodded with encouragement as she collected the projects to display on the wall. When it was Max's turn, he exuberantly shared that he was proud of how he colored his project and added the stem and leaf.

"And my favorite part about my project," Max said with pride, "Is that I did it all by myself." Ms. Henning started the applause and the group gave Max a hearty cheer for his efforts. Jamie felt her heart warm in her chest as she realized with relief that Max's project was absolutely fantastic because it was HIS OWN. She also realized that being a parent isn't about putting on a good show for anyone else or trying to be perfect. It was about loving her son, providing for him, and doing what she could to help school be a successful place.

Perhaps you have been there. Like Jamie, you have had the sinking feeling that you are forgetting something only to realize that yes, it's true, you have dropped the ball. As parents, we are in a constant juggling act which tends to ebb and flow based on the demands of life and the needs of our children. One thing I can promise you is that yes, you will indeed drop the ball at times. And guess what? It's completely okay. Everything tends to work out one way or another and expecting yourself to be perfect is a one-way ticket to stress, stress, and more stress.

This chapter will focus on how you can let go of the need to be perfect or to be a constant savior for everyone in your life. At times, in fact, it's important to put yourself first if you intend to be your best for others. This isn't selfish, it's necessary. This chapter will help you give yourself permission to take good, loving care of YOU. It will include the opportunity to develop strategies to deal with your most prominent stressors, as well as approaches you can take to be gentle and kind with yourself. This chapter will also help you better protect your time and energy through the development of routines and boundaries. The hope is that you will grow in your ability to balance giving to others with caring for yourself so that you don't collapse into stress and burnout. Trust me, if you don't invest the time in caring for yourself, you won't have as much to give to others. You can't pour from an empty cup.

Key Themes

♦ Give yourself permission to let go of perfectionism, worry, and comparison which can lead to stress and burnout.

♦ Identifying your most prominent stressors and your go-to solutions can help you manage difficulties more effectively.

♦ Self-kindness is a powerful tool to sustain yourself and find health and wholeness for the betterment of your life and the life of your child.

♦ Developing and utilizing routines can be extremely helpful for all members of your household and can support school success.

♦ Establishing boundaries to protect your energy is critical to your overall health. You can't do it all, and this is okay!

♦ At any moment you can shift your thinking from stress and struggle to peace and calm through strategic approaches.

Put Yourself First

Imagine you are flying on an airplane. The flight attendant is going over the safety rules and regulations prior to takeoff. There is one common message which is shared universally in such situations: In case of emergency, secure your own oxygen mask before assisting your child in utilizing their own. Why? Because unless you are breathing, you can't help your child breathe. What does this mean for you as a parent? It means that you need to take good, loving extravagant care of yourself if you want to be your very best self for your child. This doesn't make you selfish and it shouldn't be a source of guilt. Meeting your own needs first is actually an act of love because you can't pour from an empty cup. Trust me, I've tried over the years!

There is one mistake far too many parents of children with special needs make: they neglect self-care and their personal time and allow parenting to take over all aspects of their being. As so many of us have learned, the role of a parent can EAT YOUR LIFE. In fact, the more you love your child and the more you care, the greater the danger that this love will usurp your very existence. Yes, love your child. Yes, give your heart to parenting every day. Yes, this means you must learn and practice the maintenance of boundaries to establish and sustain a healthy balance. You must care for yourself as you care for your child. This chapter is loaded with practical, enjoyable activities to support you in setting boundaries, managing stress, finding wholeness, cultivating inner peace, and letting go of struggle. This may sustain you in your work and your life in general.

> The healthier you are as a person, the less you will struggle as a parent. It's as simple as that.

Anyone who enters the journey of parenthood is someone I can respect. You are a gift to your child or children, although they may never let you know this. So value yourself and take good, loving care of your mind, heart, body, and soul as much as you can. The healthier you are as a person, the less you will struggle as a parent. It's as simple as that. Children are incredibly perceptive. They can sense our best-hidden negative emotions, and I truly believe it can raise the stress level in the home. Finding your own deep sense of inner peace and taking confidence in who you are can help you create a calm, relaxed home environment in which children can best grow and develop. They in turn carry this peace with them to school to bolster their learning.

As a parent, you must find the answer to the question: What makes you happy? What's your cup of tea? What puts a skip in your step? What floats your boat? For me, it's a series of obvious, perhaps cliched habits which just seem to work. I drink lots of water. I practice yoga (I know— it's not for everyone and some of you just rolled your eyes). I get out in nature. I read books for fun and not just books about parenting or pedagogy. I drink good coffee with wonderful people who make me feel good. I work out as hard or as gently as I want, as long as I'm moving my body as often as I can. These are just a few examples and I'm not suggesting we all become yoga masters who read hundreds of novels… I'm just saying that you do well when you figure out your happy place and you get yourself there often enough to keep yourself centered, strong, and smiling. For a close friend of mine, it's the golf course. For another, it's the volleyball court. For yet another, it's reading literature featuring vampires and cheesy romance. For another, it's knitting. Yes. Knitting. Whatever your outlet, may you find it and enjoy it! Again, the more you love your life, the easier it will be to love and support your child.

Permission Slips

Flexibility is a saving grace for us as parents. This has been well-established in other chapters and I'm sure in your life experiences. Just as it helps to be flexible and gracious with our children, there are many benefits to offering this same flexibility to ourselves. There was a time in my life when I was plagued by one of the most dangerous and exhausting habits a parent can face: Ruminating. I was the queen of all ruminators and I obsessed over every little thing, especially my own actions and potential mistakes. I would replay every word I spoke in a conversation thinking, 'I wish I wouldn't have said that,' or 'I should have said _____ instead.' If my child had a tough day or there was a negative incident, I would overthink my part in the chain of events looking for where I might be to blame. It was as if I was seeking out my own imperfections and over-analyzing them.

> Rumination is an unhealthy indulgence which focuses on the negative, creates stress, and leads to burnout.

If you identify with this habit, I beg of you to please STOP! There is a vast difference between reflection and rumination. Reflection is a healthy practice which invites you to think about what went well and what went not-so-great so that you can grow and improve in the future. Reflection is positive. Rumination is an unhealthy indulgence which focuses on the negative, creates stress, and leads to burnout. So please, keep on reflecting, but avoid ruminating.

For me, the two-headed monster which constantly led to rumination included perfectionism and comparison. We've already covered the problems with perfectionism, but it's also important to mention perfectionism's not-so-nice sidekick: comparison. Comparison is the enemy of joy, and it will rob you of your peace every time. Why? Because when we try to measure our own worth by comparing ourselves to others, we will either come up short or puff ourselves up as if we are better than another person. Both are unproductive, unhelpful, and a waste of your precious enemy. Unfortunately, we currently live in a culture which feeds comparison as people post their carefully curated photos on a constant basis. Sometimes it feels as if we are all working so hard to give the impression that we are living our best lives, we forget to actually live them. If you are haunted by the comparison habit, as I have been in the past, I suggest you take a break from social media. I say this from personal experience and anecdotal evidence from countless friends and students. When we take a break from social media, we naturally become kinder to ourselves because that soft whisper of comparison, perfectionism, and rumination has no fuel to feed it.

Permission Slips

I give myself permission to let go of _____

_____

_____

If I find myself worrying about it, I will _____

_____

_____

Signed:
_____
(Your Name)

I give myself permission to let go of _____

_____

_____

If I find myself worrying about it, I will _____

_____

_____

Signed:
_____
(Your Name)

If you catch yourself falling down the rumination, perfectionism, or comparison spiral, it may be time to shift your thinking. In these moments, give yourself FULL permission to let go of the particular task or issue. See Activity 37 for a 'Permission Slip' activity you can complete to help you exercise flexibility with yourself. You may particularly consider the tasks which create the most stress or 'mental clutter.' Often, we ruminate over situations we can't change. If you can't change it, you must find a way to accept it and release it from your mind. Learning to let go allows you to return your focus to all the wonderful things you love about your child and the positive aspects of your family life together.

Pairing Stressors with Resources

Okay. Let's just start with a simple truth: Parenting your child can be STRESSFUL, particularly when supporting your child through the special education system. Stress is unavoidable in the lives of all parents, but this isn't necessarily a bad thing. In some ways, stress may indicate that you care about your child and want to create the best possible life experiences for them. Stress becomes a problem when it erodes your mental health and happiness in life. Basically, a little stress is to be expected and may even be a helpful motivator. When that little bit of stress grows into a raging monster of anxiety, it creates a toxic situation which isn't good for anyone—yourself or your child. What is the solution? Figure out what sends you into that state of stress and makes you feel overwhelmed, then identify the best solutions to combat the onset of such situations.

> Solution-based self-care will allow you to focus on the proactive steps you can take rather than the problems you face.

When you start reflecting on your stressors, it may be helpful to categorize them and identify which elements trouble you most. This can help you figure out the best strategy you can employ to deal with the things which impact you in each area. Always strive for a solution-based mindset and try not to get

My Menu of Solutions

Consider your favorite coping strategies, self-care practices and resources. These may appear in this chapter, or they may come from past positive experiences. Complete the chart to create a menu of solutions you may utilize to sustain yourself as a healthy, whole parent.

Area: Stress created by the needs of my child:	
My favorite solutions in this area:	What will this look like in my life?

Area: Stress created by my experiences with the school system:	
My favorite solutions in this area:	What will this look like in my life?

Area: Stress created by other areas of my life:	
My favorite solutions in this area:	What will this look like in my life?

stuck in the muck as you reflect on the things that weigh you down. Solution-based self-care will allow you to focus on the proactive steps you can take rather than the problems you face. As you consider your best stress-busting solutions, spend time creating a go-to menu of options you can turn to in challenging moments. Activity 38 provides an activity entitled 'My Menu of Solutions' you may complete in order to compile your favorite stress-relievers in various areas. Older children may also benefit from completing this activity for themselves. The intention is to create options you can turn to more automatically so that stress doesn't get the best of you.

Self-Trust, Not Self-Doubt

From the day you were born, you started to take in information from the world around you. From before you could remember, you received messages about who you were supposed to be, what you were supposed to strive for, and how you were supposed to act. It's called life. We are all civilized by the influences of others. Sometimes, as we grow up, we find ourselves picking up some unhelpful thinking patterns and perceptions about ourselves. We internalize the message that we aren't quite good enough so we lose touch with who we are. This creates stress and can hinder us in our ability to build up our children. Our struggles with self and identity can transfer to them, and a cycle of on-going difficulties can ensue. Self-doubt is one of the most harmful and venomous problems you will face as a parent, and if left unchecked, it could drive you into unhealthy habits or a legacy of challenges for your child.

So, I implore you, in your journey as a parent, find that true self deep down inside of you and CELEBRATE it! The needs, preferences, dreams, quirks, flaws, ALL OF IT! Being completely at peace with yourself and delving into your deep well of inner confidence will make you a stronger person and parent. This strength will carry you through any challenge you may face as you love and support your child. Stop wasting time doubting your capabilities and decisions. Trust yourself and know that

> Being completely at peace with yourself and delving into your deep well of inner confidence will make you a stronger person and parent.

you want to do what is best for your child at all times. You have much more wisdom than you may realize, and this wisdom will only grow the longer you experience life as a parent.

For many years, I struggled to trust myself in both my parenting and my teaching. I knew the parent and teacher I wanted to be, but I wasn't sure I was actually carrying out my convictions in real life. For me, I conquered this difficulty by figuring out exactly what I believed about parenting, teaching, and about myself, and then I took actions in alignment with my own heart. For example, I knew I wanted to be a parent who loved my children and my students unconditionally, but what did that really mean? It meant welcoming and accepting every single one of them. It meant putting myself in their shoes and viewing life through their eyes. It meant bringing fun into my home and my classroom so life could become more enjoyable.

Finding my true self meant I could implement a series of new and healthy practices in my parenting and my teaching. I could affirm my own children and my students for exactly who they are. I could pre-reflect on my approaches from the children's eyes and revise them to make them more engaging and effective. I could make time for humor and plan strategies to incorporate fun on a daily basis with intention. When your

> When your actions match your words and your beliefs, you find who you are as a parent and self-doubt fades away.

actions match your words and your beliefs, you find who you are as a parent and self-doubt fades away. It's a beautiful thing and it makes you fall even more deeply in love with the experience of parenthood.

Should you catch yourself falling into self-doubt, interrupt this thinking with self-encouragement and self-trust. You can always choose to cheer yourself on rather than question yourself and go down the self-doubt spiral. Own your decisions and remember that no one on planet earth is perfect, so you don't need to be caught up in potential mistakes. Think about a time when your child struggled with confidence and offer yourself the same pep talk you might have offered to them. Remind yourself that you are competent, capable, and you are doing the best you can with the resources and tools you have.

Relentless Self-Kindness

This leads to one of the most important tools a parent can employ to sustain themselves: uncompromised, relentless self-kindness. According to Germer and Neff (2013), self-kindness involves warmth and understanding directed toward ourselves when we struggle or make mistakes. If you parent for a long enough period of time, you will make a mistake which may create the need for repair. Too often, we act as our own worst critics which can result in stress and emotional exhaustion. Learning to be kind to yourself and practicing this habit on a regular basis is an act of personal care which can have a lasting positive impact on your overall health.

Too many of us spend our days being far too hard on ourselves, and this leads to a plethora of problems, including faltering confidence, inability to take positive action, and emotional pain. You will enjoy your life and your children so much more if you learn to choose self-kindness over self-criticism every time! You have the power to take control of your thoughts, and you need to root out the negative as much as possible. You can choose thoughts which are kind to yourself, over and over. Not easy, but definitely possible if you commit to this practice with consistency. Parenting a child with special needs is challenging, life in general can be overwhelming, and yes, you will rise to every challenge and sustain yourself better when you go easy on yourself!

> You have the power to take control of your thoughts, and you need to root out the negative as much as possible.

Too often, we become so lost in our difficulties that we forget that we possess a rich inner resource of personal wisdom. Activity 39, 'Letter of Kindness,' offers a structure through which you may generate advice concerning difficult situations and use this advice to be KIND to yourself! When times get tough, be with

Letter of Kindness

Consider a situation you are struggling with now or which has challenged you in the past. Imagine a friend or person you care about a great deal is in this situation. Complete the template below to compose advice to the friend. Then, re-read what you have written and <u>take your own advice.</u>

My Dear Friend,

I know you are going through _____

_____

_____

_____

You have the strengths to handle it such as _____

_____

_____

_____

Some words of encouragement I have for you are _____

_____

_____

_____

_____

Some new approaches you might try are _____

_____

_____

_____

Sincerely,

Me

yourself in a loving way and care for yourself with gentleness and self-love. Those who make this a regular practice can face all of the challenges of life with greater peace, including those involved in the work of special education.

This tool may also help your child learn to engage in self-encouragement. When your child is struggling, you could invite them to write a letter to themselves or you may co-create a positive letter together. Perhaps they would like to decorate it and post it somewhere as a reminder that everything is going to be okay. The hope is that the child will grow in their ability to cope with struggle and to exercise kindness. You might also choose to share your letter with your child in order to model self-kindness. Committing to view yourself with love and grace can result in improved mental wellness for everyone in your family.

The Power of Routine

Creating and practicing regular routines can be a powerful tool to help us avoid stressful situations. Managing the systems of daily life, such as meeting biological needs for food and rest, planning for clean clothing and reliable transportation, and other simple repetitive tasks can become draining when executed without planning or structure. Regularly engaging in practices such as exercise, connecting with others, playing, and relaxing are important for overall well-being (Weinstein and Porosoff, 2017). No one thrives in chaos, and consistent routines may become life savers in your life as a parent! It will help you so immensely if you develop and execute regular routines which set the stage for smooth sailing through the day's schedule.

> No one thrives in chaos, and consistent routines may become life savers in your life as a parent!

Specific routine activities will vary from parent to parent, but overall, those who manage the systems surrounding their day-to-day responsibilities well experience less personal stress. I must confess that I don't always practice what I preach in this area. When things get busy and I'm juggling many tasks, routine can fall

My Routines

Complete the chart to list key tasks you complete daily, weekly, and monthly. Then, add an estimated time for you to complete this and any additional notes to help yourself out!

What are some tasks I complete daily?	
Task:	Typical time and additional notes:

What are some tasks I complete weekly?	
Task:	Typical time and additional notes:

What are some tasks I complete monthly?	
Task:	Typical time and additional notes:

by the wayside and I find myself in the drive-through line more often than I'd like. It's a journey and it won't be perfect and that is perfectly okay! When stressed, the mundane tasks of life can actually provide a solace. Regular engagement in 'mindless' daily tasks can actually serve to help slow down the mind and shift the focus to the task such as washing dishes, walking a dog, or completing other basic housework or chores (Queen and Queen, 2013).

You might be thinking—YEAH, OBVIOUSLY! You may balk at the idea of reflecting on routines. I implore you, give this idea a chance. When I adhere to regular timelines for the menial tasks of life, from grocery shopping to laundry, it helps my sanity tremendously! Rather than balking at the idea of a prescribed routine, give it a chance. Knowing my simple life routines and systems helps reduce the number of decisions I need to make and I can simply walk out the steps of my day as planned. Everything gets done with far less stress than a life of pure randomness! Activity 40 offers an activity entitled "My Routines" which you can use to identify key tasks you may complete daily, weekly, and monthly as a part of the regular routine. You may also identify when these tasks might take place, keeping in mind that any schedule also involves some flexibility in light of unforeseen events.

Boundaries Are Beautiful

When I was a brand new mother, I thought I could do it all. I said 'yes' to everything and spread myself so thin, I had very little energy left for myself and often found myself in a state of irritation with my beautiful baby. I remember showing up for school at the crack of dawn and staying for long hours in the afternoon perfecting my craft, all while trying to meet the demands of motherhood. I wanted to put all of my attention on my students during the day so I saved other things (like grading, paperwork, and preparing lessons) for my personal time. I remember juggling a pile of papers to grade with a baby bottle, and the results were quite messy. I believed that this was what life as a mother was all about, imagining that I could give and give and give to my job and my child unreservedly without negative consequences.

I recall a specific moment when everything changed. I was trying to complete an individual education plan while feeding my son cooked carrots in his high chair. More carrots ended up on the floor than in his mouth and I remember a sudden, crystal clear thought which exploded across my mind: You don't have to do it all. I am so grateful for this epiphany because I believe if I wouldn't have made some changes, I may have had a complete breakdown. From this point on, I learned to say a magic word which can be challenging for many of us: NO. I said no to extra committees at work. I said no to mommy and me playgroups which created more stress by adding to my schedule. I even said no to unhelpful thought patterns like caring about the judgments of others. The freedom I found helped me grow as a parent and a teacher, and it was a beautiful thing.

Essentially, I learned to love my limits. I am not Wonder Woman. Neither are you, or Superman or whichever superhero you identify with most. If you give all of your time and love and energy to others, you have nothing left for yourself. I thought about it this way, imagine a cup, whichever is your favorite. Mine is a coffee mug which says 'Rise and Shine and Make the Day Fine' on it. Love it. The cup is filled with your love, your time, your capabilities, your attention, etc. Whenever you take care of another human being, you pour from this cup. Every time you share kindness with your child, spend time preparing a meal, run a load of laundry, assist a friend, attend an Individual Education Planning meeting, and so on and so forth. Once your head finally hits the pillow at night, you might be pretty spent and your cup might be on the empty side. How do you fill it up? Well, that's different for everyone. Maybe it's your relationships with your friends. Maybe it's cooking a tasty dinner and snuggling in under a blanket to relax. Maybe it's taking care of your pet chinchilla. As mentioned, you know the things which fill you up.

Now, here's the point. Pay attention: The things that refill your cup must never be neglected! They are absolutely necessary or you are going to burn out before I can say 'Super-parent.' Take the time for the things that refresh and restore you, and you will be better for your children. Trust me! I've learned from my mistakes. I had to find balance and learn to manage my time so that

> The things that refill your cup must never be neglected!

I could maintain a personal life even while being the best parent and teacher I could be. It's completely possible when you keep your priorities in order and stick to your boundaries. Remember that 'no' is a complete sentence, and you don't have to explain yourself to anyone.

One of the most important practices you can start now to sustain yourself is to start strengthening the parameters which help you maintain balance. I'm telling you, it is the road to happiness. Allow me to suggest some simple, practical strategies you may employ to protect your time to the greatest extent possible and invest in yourself and your family:

- ◆ If you are employed, set a 'stop' time each day and hold yourself to it! For some parents I know, they give themself an hour. One hour to either tie up loose ends after work or to think about the events of the day. After that set 'stop' time, they do not allow themselves to think about school to the greatest extent possible. When the 'Stop' time arrives, change into a new outfit! Seriously! Sometimes I also take a shower if the day at work was particularly taxing. This helps me switch into 'home' and 'relaxation' mode. Wash away the day, throw on something comfy, and focus on enjoying your evening or weekend as a parent.
- ◆ Remember the magic word NO! It is totally and completely okay to say this simple two-letter word and the earth will not crumble if you don't join every committee, plan the holiday party, coach your child's sports team, or volunteer to work at the school carnival. If you say no, someone else will step up, so share the love and don't feel you must take it all on!
- ◆ If you sometimes work in the home environment, perhaps in response to a pressing deadline, keep your 'home workspace' contained. As much as you can, keep your home a haven free from work tasks. If you must work from home, use a space which is out of the way so you

My Boundaries

Reflect on your use of time and energy by completing the chart below. Think about when you can take personal time to refresh yourself. Consider where you can say 'No' to avoid cluttering your schedule. Finally, reflect on how you can compartmentalize different areas of your life to manage the numerous 'hats' you wear most effectively.

STRATEGY ONE: My Break/STOP Time	
Time I can plan for a daily break or STOP time:	My plan to stick to this time:
STRATEGY TWO: Learn to say 'NO'	
Tasks I have been asked to do which I could say 'NO' to:	Tasks I have said 'YES' to which I could delegate instead:
STRATEGY THREE: Compartmentalization	
Concerns I will only think about during WORK HOURS:	Concerns I will only thinkabout during PERSONAL TIME:

don't have to stare at your laptop or piles of paperwork all night long.

♦ To the greatest extent possible, compartmentalize your concerns and focus on one thing at a time. For example, if you are struggling with a personal relationship, set aside these troubles while at work or spending time with your children and focus only on concerns related to the task at hand. If you are struggling with a coworker or child relationship, only think about these issues while in that environment. Try not to ruminate on problems or they will eat at you.

♦ Take a little 'break' time each day and hold yourself to it! Call upon someone in your support system to help you engage in time away from the demands of life. Even if you can only carve out 15 minutes a day, taking time to slow down, breathe, and recenter yourself will make you better for yourself and your child. A friend of mine calls this her 'B&B,' or a 'Break and Breathe.' She tends to take these moments as frequently as she needs them when she can squeeze them in. It's a lovely way to replenish the mind when challenges surmount.

In your efforts to practice a healthy and balanced life, you can use Activity 41: "My Boundaries" to create a plan to support your ability to create and maintain boundaries which can be a lifesaver!

Conclusion

Take extravagant, fabulous care of yourself, embrace yourself, and LOVE yourself! The more whole and healthy you are, the better you will be for your family. Give yourself full permission to be imperfect and to let go of things you can't control or change. Figure out what causes you stress and identify solutions to combat these triggers. Find your happy place and hang out there as often as humanly possible. Remember that your mind can play tricks on you and create problems which aren't actually there. Keep a close watch on the voice you use to speak to yourself in your head and make sure your internal self-talk is SOAKED in kindness! The kinder you are to yourself, the kinder you will be to your children.

Learn and practice the magical art of setting and upholding boundaries. You don't need to say 'yes' to everything, and if you do, you will burn yourself out. Set up healthy routines which are life-giving and support the ideal person you hope to be. If you work outside of your home, try to keep work problems at work and home problems at home. This isn't easy at first, but it's very important. Remember that putting yourself first sometimes isn't selfish, it is necessary if you are going to thrive as a parent and be your very best self. You have one sweet, precious life to live, so take good care of your one precious self!

Chapter 8 Simple Snapshot

- ♦ Give yourself permission to let go of perfectionism, rumination, and comparison.
- ♦ Identify your stressors and plan strategies to cope with them.
- ♦ Learn to trust yourself more than you doubt yourself.
- ♦ Practice self-kindness and stop being your own worst critic.
- ♦ Develop and practice consistent routines.
- ♦ Set boundaries around your energy, your time, and even your thoughts.

Chapter 8 Reflection Questions

Use the following questions to reflect on what you have learned in the chapter. You may choose to journal about them or discuss them with a partner or small group to gain further insights.

1. What are your thoughts on the permission slip tool? Where might you be able to let go of perfectionism, rumination, or comparison?
2. What are some of the most common stressors in your life and what are some solutions you may employ?
3. What advice would you give to yourself regarding the stress you are experiencing in your life? What would you say to a friend in a similar situation?
4. What are some routines you regularly practice and how do they help you?
5. How are you doing with setting boundaries? How might you use strategies such as saying 'no' and compartmentalization to help you uphold balance?
6. How well do you do with putting yourself first sometimes? Where and when might you carve out more time for YOU?

References

Germer, C.K. & Neff, K.D. (2013). Self-compassion in clinical practice: Self-compassion. *Journal of Clinical Psychology*, vol. 69, no. 8, pp. 856–67, doi:10.1002/jclp.22021.

Queen, J.A. & Queen, P.S. (2013). *The frazzled teacher's wellness plan: A five-step program for reclaiming time, managing stress, and creating a healthy lifestyle*. 2nd ed. Thousand Oaks, CA: Corwin Press.

Weinstein, J.W. & Porosoff, L. (2017). Summer self-care all year long. *Solution Tree Blog*. https://www.solutiontree.com/blog/summer-self-care-all-year-long/.

9

Help! I'm Overwhelmed

The alarm sounded at 5:30 a.m. and Lisa Nguyen decided to hit the snooze and give herself a few extra minutes of precious sleep. After talking herself into crawling out of bed, she executed her usual morning routine deciding what to wear, what to eat for breakfast and what to pack for lunch. She decided to grab an extra layer because her office was often cold. She also noticed a few notifications on her phone and decided to check them. Her mom wanted to stop over for dinner. Would she have time for it? No- she had to bring her son to soccer practice. She decided to say 'how about tomorrow?' and texted her back. Her second notification involved a reminder about a bill she had to pay. She decided she would need to pay it today, but not right at this moment. She planned to pay it first thing after work. She decided to leave herself a sticky note reminder on the counter so she would not forget. Glancing at the clock, she realized it was time to hustle. She decided to leave her other notifications for later.

She quickly popped into her son's room where he was snoozing through his alarm. Fourteen-years old, he was trying to become more independent but often needed her support and reminders. Trying to rouse her sleepy boy, Lisa decided that she had better just get going and hope for the best.

"Get moving and please don't miss the bus!" She said as she flew out the door.

Hopping in the car, she debated with herself about the best route to take to work to avoid traffic. She decided on the roundabout pathway which would avoid road work which had been creating delays. Ms. Nguyen made the last-minute decision to grab some drive-through coffee, selecting her drink and payment method. She chose to add an extra shot of espresso to give herself a little pick-me-up. By the time she had pulled into the parking lot at work, she already felt a bit tired. Why? Between waking comfortably in her bed and arriving at school, she had already made 15 decisions and counting. "Well, on with the day," she thought. With that, Ms. Nguyen headed into work to make hundreds, if not thousands more decisions before the end of the day.

Suddenly, her phone buzzed with a text message notification.

DOI: 10.4324/9781003364443-13

Mom. I missed the bus. Can u come back and give me a ride?

SIGH. Now it was time for another decision: Do I ask my boss for flexibility to go give my boy a ride to school, or do I call him in for the day because I don't have a way to get him there? She'd already missed a lot of work to meet the needs of her children and to deal with her mother's medical issues. Slumping at her desk, Lisa picked up the phone and called her son in absent. She didn't have the energy to go back and get him, and work was just too much for her to leave right now. She shot off a quick text to her son:

Can't come get you. You'll have to stay home.

'Okay,' she thought, 'Let's start the day.'

Frazzled, irritated and a bit defeated, she opened her email and started to prepare for her first meeting of the day.

Perhaps some of you are cringing at this story because it reminds you of your personal experiences. From the moment you wake up, you are right in the thick of things, making decisions and juggling demands. Life is jam-packed with decisions from the moment we wake up in the morning to the moment our heads hit the pillow at night. It is estimated that an American adult makes 35,000 decisions a day (Sollisch, 2016). I believe this is probably a low estimate when we are also taking on the roles of parents, caregivers, employees, etc. The pressure to manage it all can be overwhelming to say the least. So, how do we curb the stress of constant decision-making? Read on.

This chapter is focused on new thinking tools which will help you become a better decision-maker and so that you can declutter your mind to focus on what matters most. Working on your internal landscape can help everything fall into place more smoothly in your external life. You will explore tools to speak to yourself in a more hope-giving manner. You will learn common thought patterns which work against your happiness and develop tools to choose productive positive thoughts instead. You will learn about how systematic decision-making tools can help guide you into greater overall ease in life, as well as how

---

Key Themes

- ◆ The way you speak to yourself matters.
- ◆ Recognize and prevent common thought distortions such as overgeneralization, catastrophizing, and 'should statements' which can lead to emotional exhaustion.
- ◆ Dwelling on past struggles will do nothing for your future.
- ◆ Toxic positivity has no place in your family and it isn't helpful. Opt for authentic positivity based on evidence from your life.
- ◆ Systematic decision-making and prioritizing can alleviate stress and difficulty.
- ◆ Sharing decision-making with your child can both empower them and alleviate stress for you.

---

sharing decision-making with your child can assist in alleviating your stress. My hope is that the ideas and suggestions in this chapter create avenues for a life experience grounded in healthy thinking and sound decision-making.

Life-Giving Self-Talk

We all have a voice which speaks in our mind. It directs the path of our day and guides us along our path. Perhaps your voice is naturally kind and supportive. You believe in yourself, you are confident in every choice you make, and you never second-guess a thing. If so, you are probably the exception, not the rule. Far too often, the voice we use to speak to ourselves is too harsh, too extreme, and simply too much. This can wear us out over time. We must combat the negative messages which can play in our minds with intentional positive self-talk.

The way we speak to ourselves can come from our oldest memories. Some say that the voice in our minds will mirror the voices we heard from the adults who cared for us. If our caregivers were harsh and critical, we may be more critical with ourselves. If they were loving and nurturing, we have a better shot at being loving and nurturing within our minds. This tells us that we need to pay close attention to the voices we are imparting in our children's life experience. We can be a loving presence for them to improve the likelihood they will be kinder to themselves in the future. This also tells us that the kinder we are to ourselves, the better we may be for our children. It's as simple as that.

In order to reprogram our minds and move away from negative self-talk, we must first become aware that it is happening. At times we may not even notice that we are being self-critical or negative. This begins with the simple practice of paying attention to our thoughts and our inner landscape in order to identify our problematic thinking. Once recognized, we can choose to focus on a better thought and send an improved message. Over time this becomes a regular habit which can breathe life into your overall health and your experiences as a parent. See Table 9.1 for replacement self-talk for common negative thinking.

Another helpful practice is to start and end the day with positive messaging. Simple mantras can provide the perfect messages to get you going when you wake up. I like to spend the first 5–10 minutes in quiet meditation on a few phrases which frame my mindset in a healthy way. It usually involves something like, "I have so much to be grateful for today; I will show up and love my children today; and I have what it takes to handle anything which comes my way." I like to engage in the same practice in the evening as well. Once my head hits the pillow and it's finally time for a good night of sleep, I also return to

> "I have so much to be grateful for today; I will show up and love my students today; and I have what it takes to handle anything which comes my way."

TABLE 9.1 Replacement Self-Talk for Common Negative Thinking

Common Negative Thinking	Replacement Self-Talk
I am in over my head. I just can't handle this.	I have all that I need in this moment. I call upon my inner peace.
I always screw up when I do things like this.	I let go of past mistakes and I know I am capable.
I know I need to let this go, but I just can't seem to get over it.	All is well. Time will heal the situation. I let go of things I can't change.
If I stop to rest, I will fall too far behind to recover.	I pause, I breathe, I rest in this moment. I deserve to rest sometimes.
Maybe I'm just not cut out to be a special education teacher.	I am exactly where I am meant to be. I am fulfilling a greater purpose.

ACTIVITY FORTY-TWO

Morning and Evening Mantras

Morning Mantras:
Choose from the following list or create your own.

I will do my best today.   I am capable and strong.   I am grateful
Today will be a good day.   Today is a new day.   Today I will love kids.
I have good resources.   I am enough.   I will walk in peace today.

1.

2.

3.

4.

5.

Evening Mantras:
Choose from the following list or create your own.

I did my best today.   I let go of any stress.   I celebrate today.
Today was a good day.   Tomorrow is a new day.   All is well.
I am loved.   I am valuable.   I am at peace.

1.

2.

3.

4.

5.

the things I am grateful for. I remind myself of all that is going well with self-talk such as "I did my best today and I'm proud; I am completely at peace; and all is exactly the way it is supposed to be."

See Activity 42 for an activity entitled 'Morning and Evening Mantras' which invites you to identify phrases you can utilize to book-end your days with life-giving positive self-talk. You may also find positive mantras helpful throughout the day in times of stress.

Productive vs. Unproductive Patterns of Thought

Stress begins in our thoughts which can lead to unwelcome feelings and emotional exhaustion (Wenzel, 2019). Sounds like fun, right? Nope, probably not. Interrupting and reframing our thoughts can curb stress and head off emotional exhaustion before things escalate. According to psychologists, there are common patterns of unproductive thoughts which fall into categories such as overgeneralizing, catastrophizing, and 'should statements' (Ackerman, 2021). You can probably guess what each of these mean, but here are a few examples:

- ◆ Overgeneralization: I make one mistake and I decide that I'm a failure. I use words like 'always' and 'never' to characterize situations.
- ◆ Catastrophizing: I am constantly waiting for things to go wrong and I expect the worst-case scenario.
- ◆ Should Statements: I spend a lot of energy thinking about what I 'should' have done or said in different situations.

As you read through this list, you probably identify with some of these thought tendencies. The good news is, once you are aware of these patterns, you can make the effort to shift your thinking. Developing new habits of thought takes time, but it is definitely worth it if you are going to break free from thoughts which lead to stress.

Somewhere along the line, I learned the term 'wise mind' which refers to a way of interacting with yourself which is mindful and which leads to healthy engagement with your own inner voice (Bein, 2013). My understanding of the term 'wise mind' is that it is the part of ourselves we activate when we stop our distorted thinking and shift to what is really happening. We can have an inner discourse with ourselves in which we look at the evidence around us in our lives and realize that we are overgeneralizing or catastrophizing or engaging in some other form of unhelpful thought spiral. Then, we activate our 'wise mind' based on the reality around us. The wisest parts of ourselves want to take good care of us. We can train ourselves to turn on our inner wisdom and realize that ultimately, things are probably better than they seem.

> The wisest parts of ourselves want to take good care of us. We can train ourselves to turn on our inner wisdom and realize that ultimately, things are probably better than they seem.

Leave It in the PAST

There are two things I have found true in my experience as a parent: First, no matter how well things are going, things will never be completely smooth and there will always be bumps in the road. Second, you can learn and practice the ability to turn things around even on difficult days. I have learned that in any moment, I can stop, reflect, and shift from stuck in the muck to positive and optimistic. Optimism, or the ability to look on the bright side and expect good things, is a powerful mindset which can help us greatly in our lives. Even better? We can cultivate a lifestyle of optimism in which this becomes our natural state of being. This can take training and practice, but it is so worth it. Optimists expect the good to occur and tend to experience less stress than their more pessimistic counterparts, and extensive research supports the importance of optimism for individuals with disabilities and special education teachers (Wehmeyer, 2013). Taking time to develop the habits of optimism can set the stage for successfully 'snapping out of it' when the day is not unfolding the way we want it to.

Our brains are designed to keep us safe. It's simple biology. The brain has a natural 'negativity bias' which is a very natural self-protective measure as ancient as humanity itself (Carstensen and DeLiema, 2018). This means that our minds are constantly scanning the environment for threats and problems. This made perfect sense to our ancestors. A simple walk to gather some berries could easily turn fatal if one wasn't scanning the environment for lions, tigers, and bears. Some believe that humans are still wired this way to our very core, even though the direct threat of predatory animals usually doesn't have relevance. Unless perhaps you work at the circus or at the zoo. Understanding that the brain may be hardwired to see the negative does not mean we all have a life sentence to live in pessimism and see the glass as half empty or filled with poison.

The easiest way to resist the negativity bias is to be aware that it exists. Once recognized, we can pause and work on moving forward with optimism, bringing the good things into our awareness and letting the yuck fade away. I do this all the time, sometimes 15 times before breakfast. Not exaggerating! I have made a commitment to myself that I will not ruminate on what is wrong when so much is right in my life. I love my children, I love my work, my basic needs are met, and I am free to choose my mindset. My mental mission is to return to these truths over and over throughout the day. Negative 'stuckness' need not apply, the position of my focus has been filled by the good stuff. Is this easy? Nope! Worth it? Yep! And happily, shifting to the good becomes a habit over time.

> I love my children, I love my work, my basic needs are met, and I am free to choose my mindset. My mental mission is to return to these truths over and over throughout the day.

When a shift in thinking is in order, I have discovered that a few helpful strategies can help me get going on the road back to optimism:

◆ Chat with someone who makes you smile (or play with a pet who has the same effect on you). Perhaps this means calling or texting a friend who consistently makes you laugh. I have been known to send a girlfriend a simple text:

'Tell me something funny,' and she always comes through with a joke or a goofy piece of media. I also love to spend time with my dog. Even a moment or two 'chatting' with the pup can shift me out of negativity and into smile mode.

◆ Offer yourself a simple mantra. Grab a sticky note and write down a positive mantra to pump yourself up (as mentioned earlier in the chapter). One of my favorites for a rough day is 'This isn't as bad as you think.' I also like, 'Look for the good and you will find it.' Basically, I am persuading myself to believe in what I already know.

◆ Appreciate something or someone. Take a spare minute to send a quick thank you text or email to someone who has helped you out. Expressing gratitude helps activate the thankful and positive part of your brain. Shooting off an email of gratitude takes all of 2 minutes, and it brings a smile to both the receiver and the sender – you!

If these simple interventions don't work, it may be time to engage in 'turning your day around' through a more intentional step-by-step process. The following approach may assist you, which I call the 'PAST' strategy. This acronym stands for:

◆ Pause: Consider what is causing you to feel overwhelmed or to spiral into negative thinking. Try to find peace in your mind and body. See the grounding techniques listed in Chapter 10 to assist you.

◆ Assess: Explore the stories you are telling yourself which may be holding you back. Watch for overgeneralization, catastrophizing, and 'should' statements which are not helpful. Look at the real evidence and the facts of what is going on.

◆ Strategize: Make a plan to let go of the false stories or limiting beliefs you are holding. Ask yourself: 'What can I do to feel as GOOD as possible right now, in this moment?'

◆ Take Action: After strategizing, carry out your plan. Tell yourself that you refuse to stay stuck, and do whatever it takes to find something positive even in the most challenging circumstance.

Leave it in the PAST

You can restart your day at any moment. In moments of stress, use the chart below to practice the PAST (Pause, Assess, Strategize and Take Action) approach to resetting your trajectory from negative to positive.

STEP ONE: Pause	
What is making me feel overwhelmed?	What strategy will I use at this moment to calm my mind and body?
STEP TWO: Assess	
What are the false stories or limiting beliefs I am telling myself right now?	What is actually happening? What are the facts?
STEP THREE: Strategize	
What can I do to let go of false stories or limiting beliefs?	What do I need to do or believe in order to feel better right now?
STEP FOUR: Take Action	
How can I break the spiral of my unhelpful thoughts?	What are some actions I can take (physical or emotional) to turn my day around?

Activity 43 provides a reflective activity you might use to leave stress and overwhelm in the 'PAST.' This may also be a helpful tool to teach your children to support management of overwhelming feelings or negative thought spirals.

Authentic Positivity

Live. Laugh. Love. Choose Happy. Good Vibes Only. Most of us have seen the home decor signs which display simple phrases such as these. Some days, living, laughing, and loving come easily to us. We can 'choose happy' and stick with the 'good vibes.' Other days, we struggle to stay afloat and such didactic phrases seem to taunt us. Sometimes, you can't just 'choose happy' because your circumstances are too challenging or you simply aren't in the mood. And this is okay! The idea is that you don't set up camp and live in this negative space. The reality of life is that there will be moments of stress, negativity, and sadness at times. In these moments, no personal pep talk may be good enough to drag you out of the stress and challenge. Be real with yourself and meet yourself right where you are at.

It is important to recognize and encourage yourself in light of the significant challenges you face, approaching situations with authenticity. The term 'toxic positivity' refers to the glossing over of legitimate challenges such as stress, anxiety, and depression with surface-level solutions which do not foster resilience (Prothero, 2021). The reality of life as a parent is that there will be difficulty, there will be stress, and there may be deep pain. However, there are approaches which balance these realities with hope and life-giving practices designed to protect and preserve yourself.

> It is important to recognize and encourage yourself in light of the significant challenges you face, approaching situations with authenticity.

"Authentic positivity" offers a potential antidote to the falsehoods of "toxic positivity" through a focus on the authentic experience of difficult situations. Dan Corp, President at Advanced Time Management, offers an alternative mindset to toxic positivity which may have helpful implications for you as a

Authentic Positivity

The term 'toxic positivity' refers to the glossing over of legitimate challenges such as stress, anxiety, and depression with surface-level solutions which do not foster resilience (Prothero, 2021). Cultivate your own resilience by striving for authentic positivity instead. Complete the following chart to reflect on the truth in your challenges and to shift your thinking to genuine resilience and a healthier mindset.

What are the challenges I am facing right now? (Don't hold back, go into detail)
What difficult emotions do these challenges bring up?
What has worked in the past to overcome similar challenges?
Complete this statement and go into as much detail as possible: **I am facing (describe the challenge) and I know I can handle it because:**

parent as well as for your child (2021). It is important to maintain a degree of realism as you work to stay positive in times of stress. Corp suggests that you give yourself hope, acknowledge the struggle, and avoid empty expressions such as 'well it could be worse.' Activity 44 invites you to explore authentic positivity and cultivate your own resilience by seeing the truth in your challenges. One helpful approach is to think about times in the past when you have overcome similar challenges in order to thrive.

Wise Decision-Making

First things first. It's a common saying with a very helpful underlying message: Set your priorities in the correct order, and everything else tends to fall into place. I promise you that you will always have a to-do list in your life as a parent. Just as you check something off, something else will pop up. For some, this can feel as though you are a hamster running on a wheel, endlessly expending energy and never reaching a destination. We must combat this type of thinking in order to sustain ourselves and keep from living in constant 'survival mode.' Rather than thinking about the endless to-do list, we can set our sights on the most important tasks and take efforts to check them off. It's a great feeling to take care of priority tasks with the knowledge that everything else will fall into place accordingly.

When you think about prioritizing, it helps to realize that taking care of the most daunting tasks first may actually be the optimal approach. Taking on the most intimidating item on the to-do list may result in an increased sense of accomplishment. Trust me! I know this may sound counterintuitive. Why not start small and work your way up to the big, important stuff? I believe that the best approach for prioritization involves identifying the most undesirable, time-intensive tasks, executing them with vigor, and then leaving the 'easier' items for later. There is a natural tendency to procrastinate on the things we just don't like. Procrastination has the potential to trigger significant anxiety and worry because it involves the inactivity of piling up tasks which can lead to overload and burnout, breeding fears, worries, and anxiety (Hughes et al., 2019). Yikes. Put simply, procrastination is not your friend, even though it can seem like a lovely idea at the time. That gnawing feeling in the back of your mind is the task you are avoiding, and this can steal your peace. The items languishing on the to-do list may become like a dripping faucet, constantly present and irritating.

> Put simply, procrastination is not your friend, even though it can seem like a lovely idea at the time.

This may sound like a drag. Why would I want to complete the less desirable tasks first? For me, it's all about using my time wisely and avoiding time burglars. Carefully considering my priorities helps me stop to think about the key question: What is most important for the health, happiness, and learning of myself, my child, and my family? Whatever impacts us most is where I place my focus. From here, it can help to have a strategic approach to prioritizing. When engaging in prioritization, you can systematically differentiate between tasks that are important and those that are urgent, as originally conceived by Dwight Eisenhower, 34th US President, who once famously stated: "What is important is seldom urgent and what is urgent is seldom important" (Bast, 2016, p. 71). President Eisenhower developed a system for prioritization now commonly referred to as the 'Eisenhower Matrix' for prioritization. See Table 9.2 for examples of how this matrix may be applied to your life.

When I find myself stressed by the many tasks I need to complete and the many encroachments on my time, I sit down and draw out this matrix. Then, I complete it in as much detail as I need to in order to make decisions on how to use my time. It helps me identify exactly where my focus belongs and where it does not. I often realize that I should be delegating something that I am taking on my own, or that I am giving my time to useless activities which distract me from my goals. This simple exercise takes me about five minutes, and it can pay off in saved hours!

Over the years, I have worked with many students in special education who want to depend on adults too much. Some of them lack the confidence to take steps on their own. Others have learned that if they can get an adult to do something for them, they don't have to take the risk or invest the effort to learn and

TABLE 9.2 Eisenhower Decision-Making Matrix Example

Important/Urgent: Do Immediately	Important/Not Urgent: Schedule
◆ Schedule medical appointments for kids (due now) ◆ Finish presentation for meeting on Thursday ◆ Call plumber about leaking sink ◆ Check in with teacher – follow up from incident last week	◆ Planning for holiday party next month ◆ Prepare for meeting in two weeks ◆ Call contractor for full bathroom remodel estimate ◆ Family time/hobbies ◆ Yoga class
Unimportant/Urgent: Do Later or Delegate ◆ Organizing drawers/closets ◆ Go through old emails ◆ Clean kids' rooms or get them to clean them ◆ Social distractions (phone notifications, small talk with colleagues, etc.)	Unimportant/Not Urgent: Eliminate or Limit ◆ Scrolling social media ◆ Worrying and overthinking ◆ Perfectionism ◆ Gossip and drama ◆ Enforcing unnecessary rules ◆ Power struggles

grow. While this may be relaxing for them, the result is they learn nothing. As parents, it can be hard to hold back and help our children do things for themselves. However, we must try not to do for our children what they could do for themselves. It's that simple, and this theme will repeat throughout the book. We want to foster independence and if we allow our children to depend on us more than they need to, we will burn out!

> We must try not to do for our children what they could do for themselves.

So, consider this your invitation to let go of the need to over-help in favor of empowering your child!

This certainly applies to decision-making. Rather than making decisions for our children, we need to train them to engage in reflective decision-making on their own. Otherwise, we simply add to the thousands of decisions we need to make in a day. Also, I have found that whenever I make a decision FOR a student, they usually don't like what I decide. Although they may not realize it, they like the driver's seat and they are fully capable of taking the wheel of their own lives. Yes, even the little ones! Of course, we stay in the passenger's seat to guide them along and make sure they don't drive right into the ditch. It's a balance.

You can support your child in their decision-making skills through explicit instruction in this area. Too often, we assume that young people possess the skills to make good decisions and yet no one has ever taught them how to do this. We can equip them for improved lifelong outcomes when we set them up to make better decisions when facing a turning point or a problem. As adults, we are able to follow a series of simple steps in order to make decisions without even realizing it. This involves a form of situational analysis in which we reflect on all of the variables involved and take action accordingly. We must help our children learn to do the same.

> We can equip our children for improved lifelong outcomes when we set them up to make better decisions when facing a turning point or a problem.

This brings me to one of my favorite tools to help guide decision-making, the DBED strategy. Described in Table 9.3, this offers a structured decision-making process using the acronym 'DBED: Define, Brainstorm, Evaluate, Decide.' Once a child learns and practices this approach, they are better able to analyze situations, thinking in terms of cause and effect. Activity 45 offers

TABLE 9.3 DBED Decision-Making Steps with Instructional Tips

Step in the DBED Approach to Decision-Making	Instructional Tips for Sharing with Students
Define the decision: Clearly identify the question you are trying to answer or the decision you are trying to make.	Your child may experience stress when it's time to make decisions which can cloud their thinking. At this stage, invite them to get specific about the situation.
Brainstorm possible options: Freely list all possibilities without pausing to think them through or judge whether they are good or bad.	Brainstorming means freedom! Select the best modality for your child based on their ability. Perhaps you will talk through possible options and you could help your child list them on paper.
Evaluate each option: Review the list and evaluate whether each item might be a good or a not-so-great option. Highlight the 'good' items on the list.	Provide highlighters for your child. Support them in reading through their list and gently guide them toward the best course of action if they need assistance. Encourage independence.
Decide and take action: Select your favorite highlighted item and take action. Remember that it's okay to go back to the list and try a different option if needed.	Your child may need support in taking initial action once they have decided what to do. Help them find the first 'baby step' they may take toward the decision they have made.

ACTIVITY FORTY-FIVE

Decisions, Decisions!

Think about a decision you or your child need to make. Complete the table to walk you through the DBED Strategy. You and/or your child can use this strategy whenever you have a decision to make in your life!

D: Define the decision. What is the question you are trying to answer?	
B: Brainstorm possibilities. Make a list of all the ideas you may choose to use!	
E: Evaluate your list. Go over your list and highlight the best options. Write your favorites in this section.	
D: Decide and take action. Pick your best option and go for it!	

an activity entitled "Decisions, Decisions" which affords children at any age level the chance to implement the DBED strategy. The level of detail will vary based on student age level and capacity for self-reflection. As a parent, you might find that this strategy comes in handy as well.

Conclusion

Pay close attention to the voice you use to speak to yourself in your head. Is your voice kind, gentle, and supportive? Does your inner voice hope for the best and expect good things? If not, it may be time to create a positive mantra or reframe thought distortions. Remember that at any point in the day, you can pause, assess, strategize, and take action to turn things around if necessary. You are capable of activating the wiser parts of yourself so that negative emotions don't overwhelm you and eclipse the good in your life.

Work to support yourself and your child with authentic positivity. This means that you take a look at the full situation without glossing over the difficulties. Once you see what is happening in all of its fullness, you can take steps to support yourself and your child through the experience. Developing strong decision-making skills can reduce your stress and improve potentially difficult situations. Use the tools in this chapter to better set priorities, use your time wisely, and make sound decisions. You can share the tools in this chapter with your child as well to help them grow as an independent decision-maker. Once you have decided, stand by it and don't second-guess yourself. Be confident that you can handle anything life throws your way!

Chapter 9 Help! I'm Overwhelmed!

◆ Utilize a positive morning mantra to start your day right.
◆ Employ evening mantras to focus your mind as you are falling asleep.

- Common pitfalls of thought include overgeneralizing, catastrophizing, and 'should statements.' Reframe distorted thinking based on what is really happening.
- You can turn your day around at any time with the PAST strategy.
- Toxic positivity involves glossing over difficulties and being inauthentic.
- Authentic positivity acknowledges struggle while refocusing on resilience.
- The Eisenhower Matrix can help you prioritize tasks and manage your time.
- The DBED framework can help with decision-making.

Chapter 9 Reflection Questions

Use the following questions to reflect on what you have learned in the chapter. You may choose to journal about them or discuss them with a partner or small group to gain further insights.

1. How might the use of morning/evening mantras help you focus your thoughts? When do you struggle most with worry and stress in your thought life?
2. What is your experience with overgeneralization, catastrophizing, or 'should statements'? How might you avoid these exaggerated thoughts which pull you toward the negative?
3. What is the difference between toxic and authentic positivity? What are your thoughts on these concepts?
4. How might you prioritize the many tasks you face in your life? What are your thoughts on the Eisenhower Matrix?
5. What are some of the key decisions you have made lately as a parent? How did you go about making the decision(s)?
6. How might the DBED framework assist you in making better decisions? How might this assist your child?

References

Ackerman, C.E. (2021). Cognitive distortions: When your brain lies to you. *PositivePsychology.Com*. https://positivepsychology.com/cognitive-distortions/.

Bast, F. (2016). Crux of time management for students. *Resonance*, vol. 21, no. 1, 2016, pp. 71–88, doi:10.1007/s12045-016-0296-6.

Bein, A.M. (2013). *Dialectical behavior therapy for wellness and recovery: Interventions and activities for diverse client needs*. Hoboken, NJ: Wiley.

Carstensen, L.L., DeLiema, M. (2018 February). The positivity effect: A negativity bias in youth fades with age. *Current Opinion in Behavioral Sciences*, vol. 19, pp. 7–12. doi:10.1016/j.cobeha.2017.07.009. Epub 2017 Aug 5. PMID: 30327789; PMCID: PMC6186441.

Corp, D. (2021). When positivity turns toxic. *Grand Rapids Business Journal*, vol. 39, no. 21, Gemini Publications, pp. 18–19.

Hughes, R., Kinder, A., Cooper, C. (2018). *The wellbeing workout*. Cham: Palgrave Macmillan. https://doi-org.ezproxy.bethel.edu/10.1007/978-3-319-92552-3_60.

Prothero, A. (2021). When toxic positivity seeps into schools, here's what educators can do. *Education Week*, vol. 40, no. 17, pp. 10–10.

Sollisch, J. (2016). The cure for decision fatigue. *Wall Street Journal*. https://www.wsj.com/articles/the-cure-for-decisionfatigue-1465596928.

Wehmeyer, M.L. (2013). *The oxford handbook of positive psychology and disability*. Oxford: Oxford University Press.

Wenzel, Amy. (2019). *Cognitive behavioral therapy for beginners: An experiential learning approach*. Milton Park: Routledge, Taylor & Francis Group.

10

Gratitude, Acceptance, and Purpose

Jonelle and Anthony Smith had been waiting for this day for a long time. It was finally time to go to court and finalize the adoption of the two children they had been caring for through their county's foster care program. The journey had been arduous, to say the least, but it was all worth it to fulfill their dream of becoming parents and building a loving family. Each of their children came to them with unique needs related to their early experiences of trauma as well as their diagnoses. Over the past few years, Jonelle and Anthony had become regular fixtures at the school attending numerous Individual Education Planning meetings and additional check-in's to help the children succeed at school. It took time, patience, and love, but the school staff finally developed a plan which created a successful day for each child.

Standing before the judge, the Smith family gained two new forever members. It was beautiful, and Jonelle Smith wiped a tear from her cheek. Although the road to get to this point hadn't been easy and the road ahead would most certainly involve challenges, she was so grateful to be a forever mom. Holding the small, warm hand of her child, she gave a little squeeze as if to say, "I love you so much. This is it. You're home now. You're safe. I'm here, forever and always."

If there is one thing our children need from us, it is our consistency. They need to know that they are safe and that we will be there for them no matter what. In my life, I have found that when I view my circumstances through the right lens, with eyes of gratitude, my propensity for joy and contentment increase tremendously. This

> Being a parent offers each of us the chance to become the very best, most-fulfilled human beings we can possibly be.

DOI: 10.4324/9781003364443-14

Key Themes

◆ Gratitude is powerful and can support happiness and contentment.
◆ 'If Only' thinking works against our health and wholeness, keeping us dissatisfied in life.
◆ Expressing gratitude to others helps both individuals: The person giving thanks and the thankee.
◆ When upset, tapping into grounding techniques can help you survive any storm.
◆ Acceptance means that if a situation can't be changed, we let go of our desire to change it and find a way to make things work.
◆ Acceptance is required if we would like to find peace and joy. We cannot change and control all aspects of our lives to fit the mold we wish.
◆ Each of us is leaving a lasting legacy with our children whether we mean to or not.

---

chapter will offer tools and practices you can use to bring more gratitude into your own life and the life of your child.

Being a parent is an experience like no other. When we signed up to raise children, most of us had no idea what we were getting into. There is no way to explain the cataclysmic shift which happens when you become a parent in terms of your time, priorities, and level of responsibility. This chapter will help you explore strategies to accept your life fully, just as it is, and to thrive in your adventure with your child. The truth of the matter is, **being a parent offers each of us the chance to become the very best, most-fulfilled human beings we can possibly be**. I can think of nothing more beautiful!

The Best Job of All

Many of my friends are full-time parents and do not work outside of the home. It always astounds me that people say they 'don't have a job.' The truth is much to the contrary. These amazing parents most certainly have a job. A job with no days off, no scheduled breaks, no substitute teachers, and a 24/7 commitment. My hat is off to those who are able to engage in the life of full-time parenting. I have found balance in my life as a teacher and a mom, but I must say that the 'mom' side of my life is often the most demanding and challenging. Why? Because it's the job that never stops. We never take off our 'parent' hat at the end of the day and unwind. It's constant, it can be draining and there's no other option.

This may sound like a complaint, but in truth, being a parent can be viewed as the best job of all. We have such a golden opportunity with our little ones to infuse their lives with love, instruct them on the simple truths of life, and support them in finding their path to happiness and wholeness. At times, we will watch our children endure pain and struggle. Too often, life will make them feel chewed up and spit out. In these moments, we have the chance to give hope and bring healing and it's just so absolutely amazing. Always remember that your children are your best teachers! They are constantly communicating with their actions if not their words (see Chapter 6 for further information). Sometimes all they need is your shoulder to lean on. At other times, they need space and time to figure things out for themselves. By being there and being consistent, you are doing enough. All they really need is a parent who shows up for them.

Implement, observe, and reflect in an on-going cycle and you will grow as a parent every day. The minute we think we have the parenting role 'all figured out' is the minute we start to struggle. As parents, we do well to keep our hearts soft and open. We can allow our practices and strategies to change just as our children change with each stage of life. This process will look different for everyone. For me, it begins with patience. Be patient with yourself, with your child, and with the situations that challenge you. Sometimes there isn't an instant 'fix,' and I need to allow time and space for things to work themselves out. In the past, I have struggled with patience when there are problems. I want everything instantly remedied, but this just isn't how life works at times. Time is a great healer, and often, pausing to wait creates new avenues to solutions.

Every morning as I wake up, I take a breath and remind myself that an open, kind heart is the best thing I can bring to my children each day. If you are rolling your eyes at the cheesiness of this, I understand, but I also invite you to see what happens if you decide that your main job is to show up for your kids with consistency and love. You might just see the shift you've been hoping for. Rather than constantly 'parenting' or 'correcting' your child, they will bask in the glow of your consistent kindness and you will bring out the best in them. Just typing these sentences makes me excited to be a mom and to try to breathe life into my children as they navigate the difficult work of growing up.

Every single day I have spent as a parent, something amazing and wonderful has happened as long as I look for it with a heart of gratitude. Sometimes it's something obvious. My child aces a test or succeeds in a sport. My children are getting along and exchanging spontaneous compliments. Nothing short of miraculous. Sometimes the 'wins' are less obvious. My child takes care of something they have been putting off. A teacher shares something positive about one of my kids. Everyone made it out the door on time in the morning. My point? There is something good in every day if you look at it. We have to view our parenting lives through the lens of the positive and harvest the gold hidden in our day-to-day activity with our children. I promise you it's there. There will be times when you are bogged down by the demands of life as a parent. You may sometimes feel that you are mopping the deck on the Titanic or shoveling diamonds into a black hole. Don't believe these jaded thoughts. The truth is, as long as you keep showing up and doing your best, you are making an impact.

> Your children are depending on your ability to filter out all the negative garbage that can bog you down in life and hold tightly to the belief that the world is generally a good place and there is always something to be grateful for.

Your children are depending on your ability to filter out all the negative garbage that can bog you down in life and hold tightly to the belief that the world is generally a good place and there is always something to be grateful for. Just as an athlete engages in regular training to perform well in their sport, you can embrace the practices in this chapter to sustain a hope-giving mindset. Refining thinking patterns with a focus on gratitude, acceptance, and purpose may equip you to love your children and love yourself more deeply. A life built on love is a life to be savored and enjoyed!

The Impact of Gratitude

No child wakes up one day and decides: I'd like to have a disability. Individuals with disabilities are some of the most resilient, strong, tenacious individuals in the entire human race. They are coping with challenges they didn't choose on a daily basis. This means surmounting obstacles few of us can imagine. Unfortunately, the world can be a cold and uncaring place for those who are identified as 'different,' and our children will continuously battle stigma and marginalization. What a gift we can give them when we view them as fully capable, valuable human beings. We can make sure that they receive the message that their differences will not prevent them from becoming fully accepted, cherished, included members of the big, wide world.

> We can make sure that they receive the message that their differences will not prevent them from becoming fully accepted, cherished, included members of the big, wide world.

I decided very early in my career in special education that I would not be complicit in a system which tells students they are incapable of anything. Doggedly believing in students is a part of my daily life as a special education teacher, and I have found that students respond by succeeding. They want to prove me right when I believe in them with my whole heart, and they do. Over and over and over, I have seen students break down walls to find success beyond expectations because we both believed it could happen. There is absolutely nothing better than helping a student surprise everyone with their successes. Honestly, I live for it. And you can too, as you parent with an unshakable belief in your child's capabilities. In fact, I hope you do!

This brings us to a revolutionary idea: We can be grateful for every facet of our child's existence. We can be grateful for every strength, and grateful for every challenge. Gratitude erases frustration and helps us send the message: I am so glad to be your parent and I love everything about you. When looking at life through the lens of gratitude, individuals place their focus on what is going well rather than what is creating difficulty. Psychologically, it's been proven that people who commit to reframing their experiences from a perspective of gratitude experience more positive emotions, healthier relationships, and lower levels of stress (Watkins, Uhder, and Pichinevskiy, 2014; Wood, Joseph, and Maltby, 2009). You will be happier, healthier, and more content if you learn to start your day in gratitude and stay there as much as you can.

> Gratitude erases frustration and helps us send the message: I am so glad to be your parent and I love everything about you.

You may be thinking, 'Now wait a minute here. You want me to be thankful for things that stress me out and wear me down?' Not exactly. I am suggesting that you don't spend your time fixating on these things. Sure, negative thoughts will float by like clouds in the sky, but you can shift your eyes to the things that are GOOD because I promise you, there is ALWAYS something good going on. We can choose to see it. Gratitude is powerful, and numerous practices have been identified by research to bolster a regular mindset of gratitude including practices such as creating gratitude lists and expressing thanks to others (Ruini, 2017; Joseph and Wood, 2010; Toepfer, Cichy, and Peters, 2012). Table 10.1 provides examples of gratitude practices you might choose to use to cultivate increased gratitude in your life. It also includes possible applications for your child. Activity 46 provides a structured activity entitled 'Weekly Gratitude Journal' which you and your family can use to initiate and engage in a life-giving daily gratitude practice.

Making a regular habit out of expressing gratitude can help deepen relationships and overall positive connections for both the giver and the receiver of the thanks (Wilson, 2016; Ruini, 2017). One of the easiest ways to weave gratitude into your life more deeply is to send messages of appreciation to those who have helped you in your life. This is also a skill you can teach your child which can help them build connections and

TABLE 10.1 Gratitude Practices for Parents and Children

Gratitude Practices for Parents	Applications for Children
A parent keeps an informal gratitude journal daily focused on life events which bring joy, savoring the good in themself and their children.	At bedtime, a parent invites their child to engage in a 'gratitude check' in which the child shares one thing they appreciate about themselves, others, or an event in their day.
A parent creates a weekly 'thank you note' routine during which they write a short thank you note to another person (either in the home or in another context) who has done something they appreciate.	A child writes a thank you note or draws a picture for someone they appreciate, either in the family or in another context. The child shares the note or drawing and experiences the positive results of expressing appreciation.
A parent engages the family in sharing something positive about the week before transitioning into the weekend on a Friday afternoon. This becomes a weekly ritual to launch the transition into the weekend on a positive note.	Parents and their children engage in a weekly discussion which starts with a prompt such as, "What are you thankful for in your life right now?" or "What do you like about the way things are going?" This becomes a regular topic of conversation in the family.
During a difficult situation, a parent takes time to identify where they may be holding on to resentments or complaints which may not serve them. They spend time focusing their thinking on appreciation instead. They return to gratitude for their child or other family members.	When a child is upset, they may spend time listing their complaints about a situation and then examine each one to see how they might shift their thinking to the positive elements within their control to devise action steps. They can receive encouragement to return to gratitude after something upsets them.

grow their 'appreciation muscle.' Activity 47 offers a frame for a thank you letter you or your child could use to express appreciation to someone who has helped them. This is a more formal exercise. A more informal version would be to send a quick text or email of thanks when you find yourself appreciating someone. You will find that the recipient is pleasantly surprised at your expression of thanks. Too often, we are all too busy and focused on our own lives to reach out and share our appreciation of others.

Weekly Gratitude Journal

Pause each day to list three things you appreciate. Strive to think of new things each day to exercise your 'gratitude muscle.' Focus on the immaterial as much as possible. You can use this tool on your own or as a family to celebrate the good

MONDAY		
TUESDAY		
WEDNESDAY		
THURSDAY		
FRIDAY		

ACTIVITY FORTY-SEVEN

Letter of Gratitude

Think of a person who has made a difference in your life. Complete the sentences below and share your responses with this person.

Dear _____,

Thank you for making a difference in my life.

Some things you have done which I really appreciate are:

Some things I really like about you are:

Some reasons I look up to you are:

Sincerely,

(Sign Your Name)

Ditch the 'If Only' Mindset

From the moment we are born, we WANT something. It is completely natural. We all possess an inborn biological drive to seek out what we need. As infants, we cry when hungry, tired, or in need of other comforts. As we grow, we are constantly satiated with the concept that our mission in life is to get what we want. We ask children constant questions ranging from, "What do you WANT for breakfast" to "What do you WANT to be when you grow up?" This is natural, and there is nothing wrong with it at all. The problem is when the WANTING takes over and we forget to appreciate and enjoy what we already have.

I have heard it said repeatedly that the secret to happiness is wanting what you already have. This is such a foreign concept to so many of our children. They are growing up in a world saturated with advertisements which twist the biological drives to meet basic needs and create a hunger for unnecessary luxuries, fancy brand name items, and false solutions to non-existent problems. Parents wrestle with the same challenges, and I have seen many of my friends fall prey to get-rich-quick schemes and false promises sold by advertisers on the Internet. The dissatisfaction we all feel can result in economic gain for advertisers and yes, even scammers.

So what is the solution? Spiritual leaders have labeled this excessive 'wanting' mindset the 'if only' mind, in which individuals are unable to be happy with present circumstances because they are living in the concept that they will be happy when they receive something they don't yet possess (Coleman, 2020). We've all had the thoughts, if we are honest with ourselves.

"If only I had more money."
"If only I could find the right partner."
"If only my child would just BEHAVE."

The truth is, living in gratitude and appreciation means that we are content with everything just the way it is. We accept our circumstances and find the beauty within the mess. It can

> The truth is, living in gratitude and appreciation means that we are content with everything just the way it is. We accept our circumstances and find the beauty within the mess.

also help our children to differentiate between what they NEED and what they WANT. Personal satisfaction can be better achieved when we realize that all of our NEEDS are met, and even though we may not have everything we WANT, we can appreciate the good which is already there. Easier said than done, to be sure, but a worthy and helpful pursuit!

Practicing Acceptance

Difficult situations, emotions, and frustrations are an inevitable part of life. The worst problems of all are those that have no clear solutions. In the world of parenting, there are plenty of factors we will not like and we will not be able to change. It's just a fact of the matter.

> I realize that if I want peace in my life, I have to learn to accept the things that I just can't change and stop struggling against the things I don't like.

Being a parent will always involve responsibilities, juggling schedules, making it to appointments, connecting with the school system, etc. It will always involve challenges with our child's choices or actions from time to time. There will always be moments in which we feel overwhelmed. How do we handle the unsolvable issues and keep our hearts happy in our lives as parents? The answer for me has been **acceptance**.

In the early 1930s, ethicist Reinhold Niebuhr composed a creed which has been widely adopted by addiction intervention programs, psychologists, philosophers, and counselors which begins: *Grant me the serenity, to accept the things I cannot change, the courage to change the things I can, and the wisdom to know the difference* (Shapiro, 2014). Whether or not you believe in any sort of higher power, these words may have a powerful impact in that they introduce the concept of acceptance. When I read these words, I realize that if I want peace in my life, I have to learn to accept the things that I just can't change and stop struggling against the things I don't like. This has helped me tremendously

> Let go of the battle and surrender your desire for control, focusing instead on cultivating acceptance.

in my life as both a parent and an educator. Rather than complaining about the perennial problems which will always exist, I accept them as part of the package, and I don't give them a disproportionate amount of my energy.

The quest to resist or fight when facing unchangeable challenges can result in heartache, tension, and angst (Hughes et al., 2019). When situations cannot be changed, spend some time focusing on your inner landscape with the realization that although you cannot control what is happening around you, you can take steps to manage what is happening within you. Let go of the battle and surrender your desire for control, focusing instead on cultivating acceptance. The ability to differentiate between what can be changed in a situation and what must be accepted can be difficult. The serenity creed includes a request for discernment, or the 'wisdom to know the difference' (Shapiro, 2014). When you find yourself frustrated or facing burnout, take some time to think about the small changes you could make to improve the situation. This may help you identify the areas in which acceptance is in order because there are no current opportunities to bring about changes.

> Is this a real problem or is this a problem I have made up in my head?

So what happens when a situation is changeable? After closely examining challenging situations and reflecting on the elements which cannot be changed, you may shift their focus to the second section of the serenity creed: 'The courage to change the things I can' (Shapiro, 2014). In some situations, this is indeed an act of courage. Perhaps you realize it is time to try a new approach with your child. Maybe it's time to find a new physician or therapist to help meet your child's needs. Perhaps it is time to confront a personal issue which is encroaching on your ability to focus on your priorities and health. Maybe it's time for a critical advocacy conversation which could result in positive changes. At times, the changes have little to do with external actions and they relate to transforming patterns of thought and action which are no longer helpful. I have grown so much when

Change vs. Cannot Change

Use this form to reflect on the elements of your parenting life which are within your scope of influence and those you are unable to change. Then, reflect on the changes you can implement and how this might help you thrive.

What can I change and what must I accept?	
Things I can change:	Things I must accept:

Reflection and Application:
What are the most important items on the list of things you can change?
How might these changes make a difference to your happiness and/or health?

I have stopped to ask the question: 'Is this a real problem or is this a problem I have made up in my head?' I learned to stop creating difficulty for myself where there really was none. 'The courage to change the things I can' meant changing my mindset and my focus. Activity 48 provides an activity entitled 'Change vs. Cannot Change' you can use to reflect on what you can and cannot influence to help you practice acceptance.

Changing the Things I Can

Sometimes acceptance isn't the answer. The solution is CHANGE. When we realize that we must make a change in our own thinking or behavior, it can seem daunting. Often, we are stuck in habits of thought or action which seem to be a part of the fabric of our being. But what happens when we realize that these habits are working against us? Changing personal thinking habits or actions begins with envisioning the ideal self, exploring the strengths that will help you reach this ideal, creating action steps, and then putting them into practice (Boyatzis, Smith, and Van Oosten, 2019). Ask yourself the following questions to help initiate and solidify the changes you hope to implement:

♦ Who do I hope to be as a person?
♦ How is this thinking or behavior serving me?
♦ How is this thinking or behavior holding me back?
♦ How will this change help me grow closer to the person I want to become?
♦ How might I motivate myself to stick to this change?
♦ How can I be kind to myself through the process of change?

> Overthinking, overanalyzing, and ruminating are just worshiping the problem and giving it more energy than it deserves.

At different points in my life, I have realized that there are habits which need to change. One of these was a consistent tendency toward negative thinking, rumination, and worry. While I can still catch myself

Changing the Things I Can

Small changes can make a vast difference in your life and your parenting. Use this form to reflect on the shifts you would like to make to grow as a more whole, healthy parent.

Change I'd like to make:
Reason for this change:
Action steps I can take:

Change I'd like to make:
Reason for this change:
Action steps I can take:

falling into the 'worry' trap, I have made a concerted effort to stop these thoughts in their tracks. Overthinking, overanalyzing, and ruminating are just worshiping the problem and giving it more energy than it deserves. I have found that if I consciously stop my thoughts and even change my physical location, I can break free from worry. This effort has been worth it, and it has helped both myself and my children. The last thing they need is an anxious mother and my peace tends to translate into theirs.

At times, changes in life are more involved than a thought pattern or behavior. Sometimes we realize that it is time to move into a different chapter in the book of our lives. This may mean changes in your personal relationships, moving to a new location, or changing jobs. When life brings you a change, whether you want it or not, I suggest that you make a commitment to be extra gentle and loving with yourself. When I have faced unexpected change, I offer myself the care and love I might give to a small child. This means simple things as basic as an extra bowl of ice cream here and there, catching a short cat nap in the afternoon if I can, and shutting off social media and other distractions so I can just simply BE. Coming back to the simplicity of life can help you endure the challenge of change.

So please, when going through change, see it as an investment in your one beautiful self. Activity 49 provides an activity entitled 'Changing the Things I Can' which invites you to identify the specific change you would like to make, the reason for the change, and the specific actions you can increase and decrease to achieve the desired result. This activity may also support your child if they are seeking to make a lasting change in their lives.

Parenting with Purpose

What is the meaning of life? Why are we here? Is there some sort of master plan or great design behind everything? These are the questions human beings have wrestled with for as long as any of us can remember. The answers to these larger questions of life will vary based on your upbringing, your worldview, your opinions, and your beliefs. When I think about my own life, I know that I find a great deal of meaning and purpose in my role as a parent. What is the meaning of my life? Why am I here? To bring up the two amazing little humans charged to my care. I can think of no purpose more worthwhile and important.

So how about you? Why are you here? I believe that the moment we become parents we are charged with a new and beautifully noble purpose: To help our children fully discover who they are and how they can thrive in this world with as much independence as possible. As we support individuals with disabilities, part of our purpose is to help them utilize their strengths to overcome the obstacles they face. As a parent, this can feel like pressure and it can be overwhelming. However, when we approach our role with a deep sense of purpose, we can find ourselves more highly motivated and inspired.

As I have mentioned, I am a special education teacher. I have chosen this career field because to be honest, I find the general education setting to be quite dull and boring. I absolutely love the unique nature of students who receive special education services and the opportunity to see them leverage their many gifts to find success in life. Students with special needs are some of the most creative, kind, brilliant, enjoyable people in my life. We laugh together every single day, and I have learned much more from them than they have learned from me. For so many of my students, showing up to school each day is an act of tenacity and resilience. School has been a place of great challenge, and yet, there they sit in their seats each day. This alone inspires me to be the most dedicated and engaged educator I can possibly be. I cannot tell you how many times over the years I have turned to a coworker and said, "We seriously have the best job." We do. It's the truth. And you get to enjoy the ride as well in the role of parent to these wonderful individuals. Look for the good, the perseverance, and the tenacity in your child and you will find it.

> No matter how you landed in your life as a parent, I believe you are here for a reason. Your child was meant to be your child. Their life was meant to be in your sphere of influence.

No matter how you landed in your life as a parent, I believe you are here for a reason. Your child was meant to be your child.

Their life was meant to be in your sphere of influence. With my whole heart, I believe that parenting is a higher calling and it gives life purpose. Our children are gifts and we have been entrusted as stewards of their young lives. Everything in this book has been designed to help you fully embrace the beauty and the challenge of your life as a parent of a child with special education services. We can certainly sleepwalk through our lives in survival mode, and many people do. My hope is that this book will help you wake up to the potential JOY which can come from your experience as a parent. When you see your role as parent as part of your purpose in life, you may find yourself tapping into this joy and thriving in the journey rather than just surviving it.

> Struggles are temporary and the investment of love and guidance you are making in your child will last forever.

I encourage you to wake up in the morning with a renewed commitment to keep your greater purpose in mind. Struggles are temporary and the investment of love and guidance you are making in your child will last forever. No matter how challenging you might find your child's needs, you have the chance to breathe life into them every day and help them find their way. Consider this your mission in life. In my life, this means taking good care of myself to the greatest extent possible so that I am healthy, ready, and able to care for my children. It means focusing my priorities on my children's needs with a lens of empathy and acceptance. It also means holding them accountable when needed to help them prepare for future success. All of these goals feed into the greater purpose of helping my children carve out a life which is healthy, whole, and fulfilling.

As we finish up our journey together in these pages, I invite you to spend time reflecting on your purpose. What drives you and inspires you? What makes you feel motivated and excited about being a parent? I encourage you to return to your purpose, mission, and desired legacy when you feel the burnout creeping up on you. Stay inspired, stay motivated, and most importantly, take good loving care of yourself throughout the journey! Activity 50 invites you to reflect on the rewards you find in your life as a parent, the deeper sense of purpose and meaning you

Parenting with Purpose

Use this reflection to explore your sense of purpose and compose your personal mission statement. Whenever you feel challenged, return to this purpose and mission to help you sustain yourself in your life as a parent.

What has been rewarding about your life as a parent so far?

Where do you find purpose and meaning in your life as a parent?

What does your child need most from you?

What is your personal mission statement?

Use this sentence frame if necessary:

In order to _____,

I will _____,

because I value _____.

---

can find in the task, as well as your personal mission statement. Hopefully this tool will help you solidify your sense of commitment and purpose in your parenting experience.

Conclusion

You will fall in love with your life even more deeply when you live in a space of gratitude, acceptance, and purpose. There is always something good happening in your world, and you can 'harvest the gold' at any moment in your life as a parent. Learn to accept the aspects of your parenting journey which you cannot change and take heart that none of the problems are as daunting as they may seem. Sometimes, we discover that the lion has no teeth. The things which frighten or stress us out are actually only as problematic as we allow them to be. When you discover something you can change to improve your situation or that of your child, take action with love and empathy.

Most importantly, fully embrace your role as a parent as part of your overarching purpose in life. Recognize that participating in the parenting journey can be one of the most incredible blessings of your life if you find the beauty in every day! Realize that you have so much to offer your children and you have become their parent for a reason. Practice gratitude as a regular habit of life. Express gratitude to others who you appreciate. Explore the things you can and cannot change when you feel upset and realize that sometimes acceptance is the answer to your problems. If you can't change it, find a way to accept it and work with it to renew your joy. Finally, realize that there is a wonderful life ahead for both you and your child, and never let go of your belief in a beautiful future!

Chapter 10 Simple Snapshot

- ♦ Gratitude is powerful and there is always something GOOD going on!
- ♦ Expressing gratitude helps both the person giving thanks and the person being thanked.

- Identify what you cannot change in situations and practice acceptance.
- Identify what you can change in situations and take action steps.
- Find purpose in your life as a parent, and you will find yourself inspired!
- Make it your mission to show up for your child with consistent love, and you won't go wrong!

Chapter 10 Reflection Questions

Use the following questions to reflect on what you have learned in the chapter. You may choose to journal about them or discuss them with a partner or small group to gain further insights.

1. How might the suggestions for gratitude practices support you and your child? Which suggestions are your favorite?
2. How might expressing gratitude help you as a parent? How could this skill help your child in life?
3. What are your thoughts on the serenity creed? How might it actually help a person achieve serenity?
4. What are some elements of your life which you don't necessarily like, but which you must accept? How might you practice acceptance in these areas?
5. What are some small changes you might make in your life today to increase your happiness or bring more peace to your home? How might you implement these?
6. What do you feel is your purpose in life? How does parenting your children relate to this purpose?

References

Boyatzis, R.E., Smith, M., & Van Oosten, E. (2019). Coaching for change. *Harvard Business Review*. https://hbr.org/2019/09/coaching-for-change.

Coleman, S. (2020). Are you stuck in 'if only' mind? *Medium.**com.*** https://medium.com/age-of-awareness/are-you-stuck-in-the-if-only-mind-8198cf372f19

Hughes, R., Kinder A., & Cooper, C. (2019). *The Wellbeing Workout.* Cham: Palgrave Macmillan. https://doi-org.ezproxy.bethel.edu/10.1007/978-3-319-92552-3_60.

Joseph, S. & Wood, A. (2010). Assessment of positive functioning in clinical psychology: Theoretical and practical issues. *Clinical Psychology Review,* vol. *30,* no. 7: 830–838.

Ruini, C. (2017). *Positive psychology in the clinical domains: Research and practice.* doi:10.1007/978-3-319-52112-1.

Shapiro, F.R. (2014). Who wrote the serenity prayer? *The Chronicle of Higher Education,* vol. 60, no. 33, pp. 24–25.

Toepfer, S.M., Cichy, K., & Peters, P. (2012). Letters of gratitude: Further evidence for author benefits. *Journal of Happiness Studies,* vol. 13, no. 1, pp. 187–201.

Watkins, P.C., Uhder, J., & Pichinevskiy, S. (2014). Grateful recounting enhances subjective well-being: The importance of grateful processing. *The Journal of Positive Psychology,* pp. 1–8. doi:10.1080/17439760.2014.927909.

Wilson, J.T. (2016). Brightening the mind: The impact of practicing gratitude on focus and resilience in learning. *The Journal of Scholarship of Teaching and Learning,* vol. 16, no. 4, pp. 1–13. doi:10.14434/josotl.v16i4.19998.

Wood, A.M., Joseph, S., & Maltby, J. (2009). Gratitude predicts psychological well-being above the big five facets. *Personality and Individual Differences,* vol. 46, no. 4, pp. 443–447. doi:10.1016/j.paid.2008.11.012.

For Product Safety Concerns and Information please contact our EU
representative GPSR@taylorandfrancis.com
Taylor & Francis Verlag GmbH, Kaufingerstraße 24, 80331 München, Germany

www.ingramcontent.com/pod-product-compliance
Ingram Content Group UK Ltd.
Pitfield, Milton Keynes, MK11 3LW, UK
UKHW021429080625
459435UK00011B/213